"A thoughtful and actionable guide for Black girls and women navigating a wide range of feelings and experiences with support, affirmation, and resilience."

> —**Jamia Wilson**, author of *Young, Gifted and Black*; *Step Into Your Power*; and *This Book Is Feminist*

"This has been my experience! An excellent workbook for black girls and young women! I certainly could have used this growing up! Will be using the workbook as I mentor young, Black girls. Loved the format—could relate to all of the stories. Understanding potential meanings behind the experiences and having a plan for what to do about them—invaluable! A boy's version for my two younger brothers?"

> —**Sydney Leigh Payne**, honor student and STEM scholar at Spelman College in Atlanta, GA; mathematics major on a premed track; scholar; social and political activist; community volunteer; mentor; tutor; and musician

"*Finding Her Voice* engages Black girls in an intimate conversation about the multilayered realities of racism. It blends evidence-based research with African-centered wisdom, cultural heritage, and practical strategies. The real-life experiences and reflection exercises acknowledge difficult emotions while strengthening inner resources and support networks, including ancestors, family, and community organizations. This book can help Black girls stand strong in their identity while facing a world that often disaffirms their relevance."

> —**Sandra Y. Lewis, PsyD**, professor of psychology and director of African American Studies at Montclair State University, and author of *Life in 4-Part Harmony*

"*Finding Her Voice* is a much-needed piece of work for Black girls everywhere! As a mom of two daughters who were educated in predominantly White schools, each section of this workbook resonated profoundly. The scenarios are accurate and the activities intentional. Having access to this resource years ago would have been beneficial throughout my parenting journey with my own daughters—especially during those adolescent years."

—**Michelle C. Bair, MSW**, assistant director of TRIO programs at
Virginia Commonwealth University

"As someone who has worked closely with groups of Black girls in school settings, this book was a breath of fresh air! A comprehensive guide to being a young, Black girl in today's society. I wish there was something like this when I was younger. It speaks directly to subjects that my girls struggle with every day. I definitely plan on using it with my group once it's released!"

—**Jennifer Hall**, coordinator for Color of Brilliance girls group

"This book will save lives. It's the long-overdue guide that Black girls deserve in White spaces. This book makes structural what many Black girls may wrongly interpret as personal failings. White mothers, like me, can learn so much from reading this book and understanding how our blinders can lead us to bump up against Black girls and do real harm. Once we know, we can do better; this book makes that chance possible."

—**Courtney E. Martin**, author of *Learning in Public*

"*Finding Her Voice* is an incredibly thoughtful and comprehensive collection of powerful resources and tools for Black girls living and learning in predominantly White spaces. Authors Patton, Belgrave, and Belgrave get at the heart of girlhood and adolescence—to belong and be loved for one's true self. Foundational, contextual, and historical information and concrete action steps create a guide for positive identity development and self-advocacy."

> —**Laura Haskins**, head of school at Orchard House School

"Truly an amazing work that sensitively broaches the unique problems of Black girls through interactive activities, heartfelt stories, and educational takeaways. If you need a book that will bring a new light on your inner self and outer world, then I suggest this experience."

> —**Genisus Holland**, student at George Mason University, and advocate for rights of Black girls

finding her voice

how black girls in white spaces can speak up & live their truth

FAYE Z. BELGRAVE, PhD
IVY BELGRAVE
ANGELA PATTON

Instant Help Books
An Imprint of New Harbinger Publications, Inc.

Publisher's Note

This publication is designed to provide accurate and authoritative information in regard to the subject matter covered. It is sold with the understanding that the publisher is not engaged in rendering psychological, financial, legal, or other professional services. If expert assistance or counseling is needed, the services of a competent professional should be sought.

Library of Congress Cataloging-in-Publication Data

Names: Belgrave, Faye Z., author. | Patton, Angela, author. | Belgrave, Ivy, author.
Title: Finding her voice : how Black girls in White spaces can speak up and live their truth / Faye Belgrave, Angela Patton, Ivy Belgrave.
Description: Oakland, CA : Instant Help Books, [2021]
Identifiers: LCCN 2021006587 | ISBN 9781684037407 (trade paperback)
Subjects: LCSH: African American teenage girls--Juvenile literature. | African American teenage girls--Social conditions--Juvenile literature. | Self-esteem in adolescence--United States--Juvenile literature. | Microaggressions--United States--Juvenile literature. | Racism--United States--Juvenile literature.
Classification: LCC E185.86 .B37793 2021 | DDC 305.235/20896073--dc23
LC record available at https://lccn.loc.gov/2021006587

Printed in the United States of America

23 22 21

10 9 8 7 6 5 4 3 2 1   First Printing

This book is dedicated to all the Black girls who inspired us to write this workbook and all the Black women on the front lines of supporting Black girls.

contents

Section 3: Relationships

Section 4: Institutions

dear brilliant black girl

Yes, you! Can I tell you something? I was backstage at the White House nervously reading over my opening speech. My heart was beating so loudly I was sure that everyone could hear it. As my legs shook in my favorite pink heels, a friend texted me the encouraging words of Maya Angelou paraphrased from the poem "Our Grandmothers." I read: *I come as one, but I stand as 10,000.*

Have you ever entered a space and felt your heart quicken as you saw not one person who looked like you? Maybe you have felt like you were being judged unfairly because of the color of your skin. Have you thought to yourself, *Will people even listen to all the important things I have to say?* I have. The truth is…I still feel nervous before big events!

When I read "I come as one, but I stand as 10,000," I remember my ancestors, especially the Black women, and all those who have supported me throughout my life. Each Brilliant Black Girl descends from a long line of powerful Black women. They stand with us. Brilliant Black Girl, there are people around you who want to support you as you live out your dreams! Always remember that wherever you go, you are never alone. One definition of "brilliant" refers to color…it means shining, radiant. Trust and know that your unique gifts and talents brighten every space you enter.

President Barack H. Obama appointed me to serve as Assistant Director of the White House Initiative on Educational Excellence for African Americans. I was responsible for leading #AfAmWomenLead, an initiative launched to affirm and celebrate the brilliance of Black girls while working to address the needs of Black girls, in both policy and practice. Nearly 1,000 Black girls and hundreds of stakeholders and caring adults attended AfAmWomenLead summits. It was an honor to provide a platform for Black girl genius!

I have worked with Black girl geniuses like Marley Dias, Founder of #1000BlackGirlBooks, and Marsai Martin, an actress on ABC's *black-ish*, to lead a reading party for 250 Black girls to celebrate sisterhood and a love of reading. I've also worked with Jordan West, founder of Princess for a Day, which hosts a Princess for a Day party for girls of color who are homeless or in foster care.

Finding Her Voice: How Black Girls in White Spaces Can Speak Up and Live Their Truth
is the workbook I wish I had when I was younger! This book was created by three
incredible experts to help you recognize and address some of the challenges you may
experience as a Brilliant Black Girl. Dr. Faye Belgrave, Angela Patton, and Ivy Belgrave
will be with you as you work through the activities designed to help you realize your
dreams. The workbook features the stories of other Black girls just like you as they
work to find their voices.

There's no wrong way to complete this workbook. You can pick up your pen or pencil
and start here at the beginning and complete the activities in order, or, if you prefer,
you can work on whatever activity speaks to you wherever it is located in the book.
You can do it alone or with your support squad. (Flip to Activity 17 if you need help
identifying or building a strong social support system). This book is a tool, and it's
meant to be used again and again. Make sure to keep it in a special place so you can
always come back to your favorite sections or redo your favorite activities.

I'm excited for your journey and I'm so proud of you! Shine on!

With love,

Dr. Lauren Mims

welcome

Have you experienced stress, frustration, self-silencing, anger, or sadness as a Black girl attending a predominantly White school? Maybe you have been the only Black voice in a social situation. Maybe you have felt lonely as the only Black person in a group. Or maybe you have experienced subtle discrimination. However, you have taken an important step toward self-empowerment and taking control of your feelings and experiences by choosing to use this workbook. By reading situations faced by other Black girls in White spaces and responding to critical questions and exercises, you will learn to recognize and address some of the challenges unique to the Black girl experience.

The authors of this book will be your guides on this journey. Here's who we are:

Dr. Faye Belgrave. I support Black girls in developing the confidence and skills to realize their dreams by tapping into their culture and their individual strengths. I am a professor of psychology.

Angela Patton. I want Black girls to visualize their bright futures and potential through discovery, development, innovation, and social change in their communities. I am the chief executive officer of an organization focused on advancing Black girls.

Ivy Belgrave. I run groups for Black girls to support them in White school settings, helping them thrive academically and socially. I have been a teacher for many years.

The three of us have all seen the challenges Black girls face. We have talked to teen girls and young adults who have successfully navigated difficult situations, and we have included their stories in this book. Most importantly, we have lived many of the experiences and the situations represented in this book.

plan for using this workbook

Let's make a plan for how you will use this workbook. Your plan should include all the items listed on the scroll on the facing page. There are twenty-six activities. Ideally, you could do one activity a week, but you might want to finish more quickly and do more than one. It is up to you. The most important thing is that you work at a pace that is manageable and meaningful to you.

a journey to yourself

We have three goals for you by the end of this workbook.

- **You are seen.** We see all the amazing parts of who you are. Some may call it Black girl magic, but it's not magic. It's just your light shining through.

- **You are knowledgeable.** We want you to learn about yourself and the community of Black girls with your shared experiences.

- **You are empowered.** We want you to feel ready to face the challenges heading your way.

So let's get going!

My Plan for Learning How to Find My Voice and Be My True Self

I would like to learn _____

I will ask _____ to read this workbook
        [name of person]

with me. Or, I will ask _____ if I have
                    [name of person]

questions and want to discuss what is in this workbook.

I will read an activity from this book (circle one)

   Daily   *Weekly*   *Monthly*

I commit to doing the activities in this book.

Signature   Date

_____   _____

SECTION 1

Identity

1 black girls face challenges in white spaces

Nia has enjoyed swimming since she was five. At fourteen, she is excited to be on a citywide team for the first time. She and her parents were very proud when she made the team. The twelve-member team is composed of girls between the ages of thirteen and fourteen. Most of the other girls on the team have been together for three or four years. Nia is the only Black on the team. All the other girls are White. Several of the other girls live in the same neighborhood. Nia lives across town.

The swim team has a meet in a few days. Nia is excited about the meet. She is confident in her skills. The coach has chosen her to anchor her teammates in a relay, proof that she is a valuable member of the team. In the locker room a few days before the meet, Nia overhears her teammates discussing a party being held after the meet. "The party's at Emily's house"; "We invited some kids who aren't on the team"; "That cute boy Joe said he'd come."

Nia had not heard anything about the party. It is surprising because all the girls seem nice to her. Her parents seem to get along with the other girls' parents. Nia has even been out with Hannah and Taylor a couple of times after practice. Nia's first reaction of surprise quickly turns to anger, then sadness. She wants to be a part of this team in every way. She thinks about it all the way home. Why was she not invited to the party? Is it because she has been on the team for only a short time? Is it because she does not live in the same neighborhood as the other girls? Or is it because she is Black?

for you to know

Predominately White spaces—most of us have been in one. Have you entered a class or other event and saw not one person that looked like you? Maybe it's on the court with your basketball team, in your neighborhood, at the mall, or the school you attend. When you're in a White space…

- Have you ever been stereotyped as loud, aggressive, or defiant?

- Do you feel that teachers have lower expectations of you?

- Do you feel that rules and consequences are stricter for you than for girls of other racial groups?

- Do you sometimes feel unsure about adults' intentions toward you?

Do you wonder if these things happen because you are Black? What about when a topic about Blacks comes up in conversation and others look at you to speak? If any of these sound familiar, this workbook is for you.

In predominantly White spaces, these experiences may silence you and you may pretend there are no problems. While pretending, you may feel stress, anger, sadness, and isolation by not speaking up and living your truth. When you do not live your truth, you miss out on positive experiences with your peers, teachers, and others. You limit learning opportunities, activities you would like to participate in, and people you might want to get to know. Acknowledging these experiences is the first step in learning how to deal with them.

If this is your reality, acknowledging it will help you in dealing with some of the challenges you might face. We discuss these challenges and provide activities to help you think about the best way to respond. You may have a mix of positive and negative experiences in White spaces. If this is the case, your positive experiences will help you balance out challenging ones.

for you to do

Sometimes, when we feel excluded, we are not sure why. Why do you think Nia was excluded?

_____

_____

_____

Have you ever felt excluded and not known the reason why? Write down what happened to you.

_____

_____

_____

Now describe how you felt.

_____

_____

Feeling excluded can bring up all types of emotions—loneliness, sadness, hurt, and even anger. If you keep these feelings to yourself, an incident of exclusion will continue to bother you. Therefore, it is important to get another person's perspective. In the circle below, list all the people you think can help you if you encounter situations where you feel excluded. Start with those you might be closest to, such as a parent, friend, or sibling. Write their names in the circle outside the circle with the word "me." Then think about others you see on a regular basis—perhaps a teacher, a neighbor, or a coach. Put their names in the outer circle. Both these groups will be your support team.

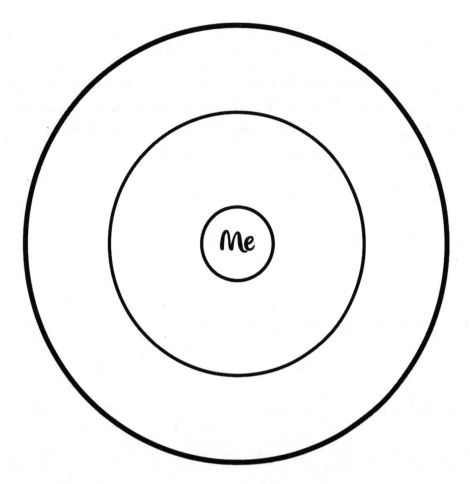

Now that you have your support team identified, set up a time to discuss with one person the situation you wrote about, when you were excluded. Don't forget to let the person know how you felt. Talking to someone about being excluded can be helpful. It will validate what you experienced and felt and give you another perspective. It reaffirms that you are supported by many people who want to include you in their lives.

more to do

Most teens, regardless of race, will face some exclusion. However, there are many groups you *are* included in. They may be groups in schools, religious institutions, or recreational and athletic clubs, among others. If you are not already in one, identify a Black girls' group to join. The group can meet in person or online. Research the group before you join to make sure it is a positive one. Focusing on groups you belong to rather than those you are excluded from will make you feel better.

One Black girls' group I would like to be a part of is

_____

The first step I will take toward joining this group is

_____

_____

microaggressions are harmful

2

Kamila, a thirteen-year-old Black teen, lives in a predominantly White neighborhood. She has many neighborhood friends and has always liked where she lives. One Halloween, she takes her eight-year-old brother trick-or-treating. Her parents told her that they could go throughout the neighborhood. Kamila and her brother ring the doorbell of a house they have not been to before. The woman who answers the door is pleasant and generously provides them treats. And then the woman asks, "What neighborhood do you live in?"

Kamila feels that something is not right but she cannot immediately identify what it is. She assumed that since only children who lived in her neighborhood went trick-or-treating there, the woman would know she lived nearby. Kamila has conflicting thoughts. The woman had sounded polite when asking the question. She had been pleasant and provided generous treats. But Kamila has a nagging feeling about the question. Did this woman not expect a Black family to live in their neighborhood?

for you to know

Kamila experienced a microaggression, which is an everyday slight, putdown, or insult. Microaggressions are directed at people based on disability, gender identity, sexual orientation, race, ethnicity, nationality, or religion. You are not always aware of microaggressions or that the message was intended to be hurtful. You may feel insulted, but often you feel that something is just not right. Like the name suggests, *micro* means it can be a very small thing. However, it may appear small to an outsider, but to you, it doesn't feel small.

Microaggressions can be verbal or nonverbal. An example of a nonverbal microaggression is when your teacher does not call on you when you raise your hand. A verbal microaggression is, for example, when someone fails to correctly pronounce your name after being corrected.

Microaggressions can also be intentional or unintentional. An unintentional microaggression might be if someone asked, "What are you ladies gossiping about?" implying that when Black girls talk they are gossiping. An intentional microaggression might be being told that you don't have the qualifications to be part of a program when you do.

Check the box next to each situation that has happened to you.

☐ A salesclerk followed you around in a store.

☐ Someone acted surprised when you told them you are in an advanced course.

☐ Someone from another racial group tried to touch your hair.

☐ A person told you that you were chosen to be in a program because of your race.

☐ You heard someone say they do not want to live in or attend school in a Black neighborhood.

☐ You were searched at an event when others were not searched.

☐ You were told you should not wear braids or locs to an event.

☐ Someone told you that you are pretty for a dark-skinned (or big) girl.

If any of these have occurred, you have likely experienced a microaggression. Unfortunately, most Black people experience several each day.

for you to do

Microaggressions do not just hurt your feelings. They have other damaging consequences on your mental and physical health because of the ongoing stress they cause. You exert time and energy thinking about them. Therefore, it is important for you to recognize microaggressions and learn how to respond to them. Sometimes the best response is to confront the person, other times it may be to get help from an adult or peer, and sometimes the best course of action is to ignore the microaggression.

These pictures show a teen who has experienced microaggressions. Under each picture, write down one or two words that might express her feelings.

_____   _____   _____

_____   _____   _____

Have you experienced a microaggression, either from the list above or another microaggression? Describe your experience.

_____

_____

_____

_____

In the box below, draw a picture or write words or sentences that express how you felt.

more to do

Think about how you could respond to a microaggression. For example, what would you do if a salesclerk followed you around in a store? You could leave the store and not shop there again. You could tell the clerk that you will let them know if you have questions. This may be difficult at first, especially if the person is an adult. But when you practice, you will get better at it. Write down some of your ideas here:

_____

_____

_____

You could also talk to an adult about how to respond. Write down some of the things you will talk about here:

_____

_____

_____

Remember, the more you practice, the more confident you will feel. And the more confident you feel, the less stressful the experience will be. Also, keep in mind that you do not have to respond to every microaggression. Just recognizing microaggressions for what they are makes them less stressful. You know that it is not about you but the ignorance of the person making the microaggression.

what is racial identity?

Amelia sits down, nervously. She has never been called to visit the guidance counselor and wonders why she was pulled out of study hall to do so now.

"I bet you're wondering why you are here," Mrs. Jeffries begins. Amelia nods, wishing she would get to the point.

"Well, Amelia, I was going over your application for the Summer Science Institute at the Smithsonian." Amelia lets out a silent sigh of relief. "I noticed that you declined to answer the question about your race. Quite frankly, I think you should tell them that you are Black. It could really improve your chances of being accepted. The program is committed to diversity, and your race would be an asset."

Amelia sits there silently. She doesn't want to identify herself as Black just to get into a program. Amelia goes to an excellent private school. Her mother is a doctor, and her father, a university professor. Amelia is not naive to the plight of many Black Americans. Her parents have always reminded her of how many more opportunities she has than most Black people. When programs are "committed to diversity," aren't they talking about a different kind of Black?

"I'll have to think about it, Mrs. Jeffries," Amelia says as she gets up to leave. Amelia has to think about a lot. What exactly is being Black, beyond the shade of her skin?

for you to know

Imagine you live in a racially diverse city; however, all the professionals and businesses you visit are White: your pediatrician, dentist, dance teacher, chemistry tutor, and more. Additionally, the stores you shop in, the school you attend, and the neighborhood you live in are predominately White.

Now imagine yourself visiting a racially mixed group of professionals. Some are Black, some White, and some members of other racial and ethnic groups. Does it feel different to go to businesses that are owned by Blacks and events that are organized by Blacks? It likely feels more supportive and encouraging to be around professionals who look like you.

The second situation lends itself to a stronger racial identity than the first. Racial identity is how you feel about your racial group. Our parents influence our racial identity the most as they model what to say and do regarding race.

Strong racial identity is feeling proud to be Black and is a good thing to have. Girls with a strong racial identity tend to do better socially and academically. You are likely to have higher self-esteem and value yourself more than those with a weak racial identity. Acknowledging and feeling good about who you are makes you better equipped to deal with some of the microaggressions and problems Black people encounter.

People with strong racial identities are not anti-White or anti any other racial or ethnic group. You can have a strong racial identity and have positive relationships and activities with people who are not Black. Your racial identity has to do with how you feel about yourself.

Having a strong racial identity means recognizing that there is no single way to be Black. It also means understanding that as a Black person you have a shared history and experiences with other Black people. It is also about your behaviors, including visiting Black businesses and using Black professionals if possible.

If you are a Black girl in a White space, having a strong racial identity may not come automatically. After all, you spend a lot of time in White spaces and may not be around other Blacks, including your peers and teachers. There are things you can do to strengthen your racial identity, but first let's explore what it means to you now.

for you to do

Why do you think Amelia did not want to identify her race on her application?

_____

_____

_____

Do you think programs focused on racial diversity are helpful to Blacks? Why or why not?

_____

_____

_____

Sometimes when we are in White spaces, we may not want our race to be the most noticeable thing about us. If you are like most teens, you want to fit in and be like your peers. We encourage you to acknowledge your race as a first step to forming a healthy racial identity.

There are many different ways to feel about your racial group. For example, you might feel ambivalent about being Black. Or you might feel proud. Or you might have negative feelings. Express your feelings about being Black below using five words.

1. _____

2. _____

3. _____

4. _____

5. _____

Reflect on why these words came to mind. Remember, your feelings belong to you, and there is no right or wrong way to feel. Try putting them into a sentence that expresses what it means to be Black.

Being Black makes me feel _____

_____

_____

_____

_____

more to do

Think about how you can positively express your racial identity. For example, you could write a poem for a class on what it means to be a Black girl in America. You could go to a movie with a Black actress as the lead. You might wear a T-shirt or hat with a pro-Black slogan, from "Melanin Blessed" to "Black Lives Matter."

How would you express yourself by wearing a T-shirt with a positive Black message? Using the shirt on the facing page, design your own image and slogan.

Engaging in behaviors that support your positive racial identity will make it more noticeable and relevant to you. Just remember that you have to practice expressing your identity in an ongoing way. This is a lifelong process, and one with many rewards.

4   strengthening your racial identity

Gia's family has a tradition of eating at Aunt Mae's Soul Food Kitchen every Sunday. It is a restaurant known for excessively long wait times, mediocre service, and the best fried catfish and mixed berry cobbler known to mankind. As soon as they changed out of their Sunday best, Gia and her family would order a mini-feast to bring home and enjoy.

One day on the way to church, Gia's mom asks casually, "Why don't we try that new restaurant, Southern Kitchen?"

"We can't," Gia's dad says emphatically. "It's important to support Black-owned businesses. We can't let some corporate chain profit off the creativity of Black folks. And most importantly, there is no way some chain restaurant can touch Aunt Mae's food."

Gia can't imagine anything tasting better than Aunt Mae's cooking, but she feels that her dad is being a bit dramatic. Does it really matter who invented fried okra? Her dad is always preaching about supporting our own and patronizing Black businesses. Gia doesn't see what the big deal is.

for you to know

Being in predominantly White spaces may challenge your racial identity. If you do not see any Black art, cultural symbols, teachers, or peers, you may have conflicting feelings about being Black. Perhaps you have been told that if you work hard, you will be judged by the quality of your work regardless of your race. You may be surrounded by people who claim to be color-blind, who refuse to acknowledge your Blackness at all. Or even more destructively, you may be surrounded by negative images of Blacks, especially from the media. All these factors are working to shape your racial identity.

To form a healthy racial identity, you must make a conscious effort to combat negative influences. Here is what we know about people with a strong racial identity:

- They are proud to be Black.

- They like being around other Black people.

- They participate in Black events.

- They purchase goods and services from Blacks.

- They realize they will be discriminated against.

- They do not believe any race is better than or superior to any other.

- They go out of their way to support Black businesses.

Did you notice that some of these characteristics are about feelings (like being proud)? Others are about behaviors (like purchasing goods and services from Blacks). There are many ways to develop a healthy racial identity.

for you to do

Having a strong racial identity begins with the knowledge of Black people. Our history and culture did not start with enslavement, it started in Africa. Learning about Africa will help you appreciate your Black culture.

Africa, the second largest continent, was home to powerful women throughout history—women who led their country as rulers, warriors, and developers of their country's wealth. Women who shared your skin tone, facial features, and hair texture were running things for hundreds of years. Here are some African queens:

- Queen Amina was a warrior queen of Nigeria.

- Yaa Asantewaa (Ghana) was a gifted politician and negotiator.

- Queen Nefertiti's (Ancient Egypt) name translates to "the beautiful one has come."

- Queen Moremi (Nigeria) was revered for her loyalty and sacrifice for her people.

- Queen Ranavalona (Madagascar) was known for her abundance of style and grace.

- Queen Nzinga (Angola) led troops in battle against Portuguese slave traders.

Choose an African queen, and use the internet to learn more about her. Reflect on this queen's contribution to her country. List three things she accomplished.

1. _____

2. _____

3. _____

What about her story resonates with you? For example, did her strength or wisdom remind you of any women in your life? Did you see yourself in any of her stories? Reflect below.

_____

_____

_____

_____

_____

_____

By learning more about your history from Africa, you will begin to develop racial pride. The next time a cultural event such as Kwanzaa, Juneteenth—which celebrates the day slaves officially were told they were free—or any other Black festival is observed in your community, plan to attend.

Engaging in behaviors that support other Black people will strengthen your racial identity. Talk to your parents about why this is important to you. A powerful way to do this is to be like Gia's family and support Black-owned businesses in your community or online.

more to do

Why do you think Gia's father will eat only at Aunt Mae's Soul Food and not at the chain restaurant?

_____

_____

Identify a Black-owned business in your community that provides products or services in which you would like to engage. Maybe it's a clothing store, supermarket, cell phone repair shop, hair salon, or food truck. If you don't know one, ask your parents or do an internet search. Then write down the name of the business.

_____

What products or services does this business provide?

_____

_____

Plan a visit. Invite a friend to go with you. When you patronize Black businesses, you are supporting and learning more about Black people in your community.

I am not just black, I am biracial 5

Jayla is a biracial girl in tenth grade at a predominately White school. Her father is White, and her mother is Black. She heard about an after-school program for Black girls that focuses on empowerment and self-esteem by teaching more about Black culture. She is proud of her Black ancestry and wants to be part of this group. She attends the first meeting of twelve girls. The girls all seem to be friends and are engaged in casual conversation.

However, it appears to Jayla that no one is trying to involve her in the conversation. One girl mentions a movie with a Black actress she is going to see. Others are talking about upcoming events at the school. One girl is discussing an incident that she thought was racist. When the adult leader comes in, she says that the purpose of the group is to help Black girls develop self-esteem and racial pride. At this point, Jayla feels that all eyes are on her. She does not know why, but she feels uncomfortable.

Although Jayla identifies with both Black and White cultures, in appearance she looks White. Jayla then realizes that perhaps the other girls think she is not Black. Or they may feel that she is not Black enough. Jayla does not return to the second session, although she wanted to be part of the group.

for you to know

We are now seeing more and more interracial relationships, and children of these relationships often identify with the racial (or ethnic groups) of both parents. Perhaps one of your parents is White, Latinx, or Asian, while the other is Black.

Although you identify with both racial groups, people often expect you to choose one. This happens when you fill out a form, and there is only one option for race. Or when assumptions are made about you based on the racial group you look like. Have you ever been caught in a situation where Black people think you are not Black enough, and White people treat you as if you were Black? Many biracial teens report having these challenges. How about you? As a biracial teen, you may also find yourself experiencing more microaggressions because you are more likely to be in White spaces.

If you are like most teens, fitting in is essential. Not knowing where you fit in can bring about all kinds of emotions—confusion, isolation, and stress. You may have conflicts between what you feel or believe and how you are treated. For example, you may identify as being biracial but be treated as if you are a member of the group you look like.

While you may face many challenges, you can also feel empowered by being biracial. Biracial teens interact with family and friends from different racial and ethnic groups. Being exposed to different racial or ethnic groups gives you diverse perspectives. It also will help you learn to get along with people from various other cultural groups.

Even if you do not consider yourself biracial, we encourage you to work through this activity and the next. You may find that there are other cultural identities you hold. By working through these activities, you can also better understand and support peers who are biracial.

for you to do

How do you think Jayla felt at the meeting?

_____

_____

_____

Sometimes, when we feel left out, we are not sure why. Perhaps Jayla was ignored because she thought she was perceived as not Black. Or maybe it was because she was not friends with any of the other girls in the group.

What could Jayla have done at the meeting to show interest? For example, could she have introduced herself to one of the other girls? Write down a couple of ways to connect.

_____

_____

_____

Describe a situation where you felt ignored or left out of a group because others saw you as different.

_____

_____

_____

_____

How did you feel?

_____

_____

_____

Review your response. Is there anything that you would do differently if you were in this situation again?

_____

_____

_____

_____

_____

more to do

If you are biracial, you may have been asked "What are you?" This question is rude and may make you uncomfortable. It implies that you have to fit into one category, and all your racial or ethnic identities are not acknowledged.

Now let's think about some things that you might say in response to this question. Keep in mind people may not understand that it is rude. You could reply, "I identify as both Black and White" (or other racial/ethnic groups). Or you can say, "My parents are White and Black." By thinking of potential responses, you can be better prepared, which will alleviate the stress that may come from being asked that question.

_____

_____

_____

_____

_____

You may have heard the question "What are you?" being asked of someone else. How could you respond to be an ally to that person?

_____

_____

_____

_____

Even if you are not biracial, someone might ask you about your identity. How could you respond?

_____

_____

_____

_____

Remember, it is you who gets to choose your identity as a biracial person—not anyone else. You may also want to talk to your parents or another adult about being biracial.

I am not just black, I am multicultural 6

For her fifteenth birthday, Salma's parents throw her a huge birthday party. Birthdays are a big celebration for Salma's family, whose ancestors are Trinidadian. The party is at a fantastic place, with a DJ, photo booth, and excellent Caribbean food. Her entire family comes to celebrate, along with friends from school. Salma spends the evening having a blast, dancing, eating, and laughing with all her guests. She can tell that her friends and family are enjoying themselves as well. Her aunts leave the dance floor just long enough to get another helping of fried plantain or beef patties. At one point, she even catches her grandmother teaching some of her friends Calypso, a traditional Trinidadian dance. That night, Salma goes to bed happy and exhausted.

The morning after her party, Salma wakes up and begins to check her social media accounts. A lot of her friends mentioned her party and what a great time they had. She smiles and continues to scroll through her accounts. She comes across a few posts that confuse her.

Is this supposed to be a party? The post was made at 6:50. Her invitation had stated that the party wouldn't start until 7:00. This meant 7:45 to most of her relatives. Salma thinks, *Why would you come to an event early?*

Hasn't anyone ever heard of chips and dip? Salma thinks, *Leave it to these guys to not appreciate real food. You're lucky if they serve punch and pretzels at their parties.*

I think it's past Grandma's bedtime. Salma's family always celebrates together. She loves her grandmother dearly. Why wouldn't she be there for her birthday?

Salma is shocked to see some of the posts on social media about the event. Even though responses are overwhelmingly positive, it upsets her that she had invited people who didn't appreciate her food and family. Salma wants to respond to the negative posts, but she does not know what to say. She also thinks it might be better not to respond.

for you to know

Our race, ethnicity, religion, age, country of origin, disability status, and sexual orientation, among other characteristics, define our cultural group. A cultural group has similar attitudes, values, and behaviors. If you identify with two or more cultural groups, you are multicultural.

In this activity, we want you to focus on the cultural groups you identify with. Are your parents Black and also recent immigrants? Are you Black and also a religious or sexual minority? What about Black and a person with a disability? If so, you likely have a multicultural identity. You can be bicultural or multicultural based on many configurations.

Even if you do not consider yourself multicultural, we encourage you to work through this activity. You may find that there are many cultural identities you hold. By working through this activity, you can also better understand multicultural peers.

One of the challenges of being multicultural is that people still treat you as if you belong to one cultural group. If you are Black and Caribbean, you may be treated as if you are only Black. If you are Black and have a disability, you may be treated as a person with a disability. Though you may face some challenges, being multicultural may give you an edge into different cultures and ways of living.

Blacks born in African, Caribbean, or Latin American countries have both similar and different values, beliefs, and behaviors than Blacks born in the United States. For example, a friend from an African country may refer to a friend of their parents as "aunt" or "uncle," although there is no biological relationship.

Also, in African, Caribbean, and Latin American countries, families and friends of all ages celebrate events together. In the United States, people typically attend events and parties with friends their age. You may experience discomfort when cultural differences such as this become apparent among your friends.

for you to do

What are some cultural differences between Salma and her classmates?

_____

_____

_____

_____

Do you think these differences are because Salma is Black or because her parents are from a Caribbean country? Explain here.

_____

_____

Recognizing cultural differences can help people appreciate the uniqueness of different cultures. It also prepares people who attend events with people from other cultures. Tell about a time when you felt you were culturally different from your peers.

_____

_____

_____

more to do

Now let's think about how Salma could educate people about negative posts that put down different cultural beliefs and behaviors. Keep in mind, Salma does not have to respond. Or she could say something like, "I enjoyed seeing older people having so much fun." Or "I really liked trying different foods." Salma could also invite her friends to share some of their party traditions and customs online.

_____

_____

Planning a party is the perfect way to examine some of your cultural beliefs. Not only do you acknowledge some visible cultural preferences (music, food, and clothing), you also examine some deeper cultural beliefs like relationship to time, treatment of elders, and the importance of material and immaterial gifts.

Now let's plan your "perfect" party.

Who will be invited?

_____

_____

_____

Where will it be held?

_____

What time will it start?

_____

How long will it last?

_____

What food will be served?

_____

_____

What type of music will be played?

_____

_____

What types of activities will the partygoers engage in?

_____

_____

_____

How is your culture evident in the choices you've made?

_____

_____

_____

Your perfect party gives you an idea of things about your culture that are important to you. Your culture is yours and no one else's, so own it in the choices you make and the behaviors you show.

7 what is your intersectionality?

Fatimah, a Muslim high school freshman, is an active member of her school's Black Student Union (BSU). She helps organize the meetings and is very involved in their fundraising. Mr. Kyle is a faculty advisor who allows the students to talk freely about their concerns and problems. It is lovely to have a safe and welcoming environment, even if it is only for one hour a week.

The school year is coming to a close, and Mr. Kyle suggests that the BSU have an end-of-the-year party. Everyone is in agreement that a celebration before the summer vacation is well deserved. The end of the school year is a busy time, so it is challenging finding a date that works for everyone. The group decides that a Saturday cookout would be a great way to enjoy the weather and each other's company.

When she hears the plan, Fatimah's heart sinks. The holy month of Ramadan was just starting, and she will be fasting from sunrise to sunset. She is also worried about spending hours in the sun without being able to sip water.

There are two other Muslim members of the BSU, and Fatimah wonders if either of them will mention Ramadan. Both sit silently. Fatimah has gotten used to feeling like an outsider during many parts of the day, but her BSU gatherings are one of the few places she feels welcome. If she were to mention the problems she has with the cookout idea, would the Black students still view her as one of them?

But she is not just Black, she is also Muslim. Should she be spending more time with people who share her religious identity instead of her racial identity?

for you to know

Fatimah is female, Black, Muslim, and a whole host of other forms of identity. These identities can come together in different ways, in different situations, which is known as *intersectionality*. When two or more different identities overlap to make you uniquely you, that is intersectionality.

Look at the picture. You may travel along one road, but often that road intersects with others along the journey of life.

The generation you belong to, your nationality, religion, disability status, and sexuality are all parts of your identity. These affect how you see yourself. They also affect how others see you. Some parts of your identity are seen, and some are unseen. Some parts of your identity are essential to you. Others are less important. Think about how all your different identities come together—how they *intersect*.

for you to do

Take a few moments to fill out the heart map. Each piece of the heart can have a different part of your identity. Here's a list to get you started thinking about your intersectionality.

Black

Female

American

Lesbian

Christian

Generation Z

Single-parent home

Hearing impaired

Immigrant

Now color in the heart map you made with the following code:

Blue—parts of your identity that are visible to everyone

Green—parts of your identity that are visible only to you

Orange—parts of your identity that you are still trying to define

The purpose of this activity is for you to recognize every part of your identity. Answer these questions:

Do you have more blue, green, or orange on your heart?

_____

Which parts of your identity do you feel most comfortable speaking about?

_____

Are those spaces mostly blue, green, or orange?

_____

Now think about which are most important to you. Speaking about an identity that is important to you, but not obvious to others, may be difficult at first. Although it seems silly, you may want to practice verbalizing who you are, especially about those identities that are not so visible. Some people will refuse to see you as more than a Black girl. You cannot control other people, but you can speak your truth. By expressing yourself, you will learn to embrace all of you.

Here are some examples: "My parents are from Panama, Central America, so at home we speak Spanish." "Because I'm a Seventh-day Adventist, I can't participate in after-school activities on Fridays."

Write a script and practice it a few times in the mirror. Then practice with a friend or trusted adult. Use your heart map to decide what is important to you.

_____

_____

_____

_____

_____

_____

more to do

As you practice speaking up about who you are, think about Fatimah's dilemma.

What are two identities Fatimah has?

_____

_____

Why do you think the other Muslim students in the BSU remained quiet?

_____

_____

_____

Have you ever stayed silent about a part of your identity (for example, religion, nationality, immigrant status, neighborhood)? If yes, what part of your identity were you silent about?

_____

_____

How did that make you feel?

_____

_____

_____

Fatimah can bring her concerns to the entire group or speak to Mr. Kyle privately. Which idea do you think is better? Why?

_____

_____

_____

_____

_____

Although several of your identities may be important to you, sometimes it is difficult to speak up when one is not acknowledged. Practicing what to say can help.

letting others see all of you
8

Ayla, a fifteen-year-old Black, loves to read. She spends most of her time with her nose in a book. Ayla lives in a small town and thinks of books as a way to escape the humdrum quality of her life. One of her favorite places to hang out is Shelf Control, a used-book store and coffee shop. The shop is cozy and welcoming, and the owner always recommends great books. Ayla is in her usual spot at Shelf Control when she notices the owner hanging up a flyer. The flyer reads "Rainbow Voices Book Club: Explore literature written by LGBTQIA+ authors in a safe space. ALL ARE WELCOME."

Ayla knows that this is just the club for her. She loves reading romance novels but has grown weary of the same boy-meets-girl story where everyone is White and middle class and straight. Ayla is attracted to women and wants to see herself reflected in the stories she reads.

When she looks over the reading list, Ayla sees some titles she recognizes, but she also notices that there are no Black authors on the list. There are no authors of color at all. Ayla wonders if it is an oversight. She decides to approach the owner and says, "I'm really excited about this book club. Are you open to suggestions? I was hoping we could read Sapphire or Jewelle Gomez." The owner listens, but Ayla can tell that the words aren't sinking in.

for you to know

We hope that by now, you are really thinking about how *you* define yourself. Identity is also how you feel about yourself. And while it can be influenced by others, it is also very personal. There are parts of your identity that you proudly share with the world. There are parts of your identity that you may feel less comfortable sharing. Intersectionality means that different parts of your identity overlap. You and a White teammate might both believe that girls' sports are underfunded in your school because of sexist policies. But your brother, a basketball player, doesn't think that the funding policies are inadequate. You and a Black male friend might think that the salesclerk is following you around the store because you're both Black, while a White friend may not even notice the salesclerk. Your feelings and behaviors unique to being a Black girl is part of intersectionality.

Often people will try to equate one type of oppression with another. Your teammate may say that she understands racism because she's experienced sexism. While you may have a shared experience, she cannot speak to the experience of being Black *and* female. The same is true for other parts of your identity. Often people may try to be empathetic, but when they can identify with only one part of your identity, they may not be helpful.

Unfortunately, there are always going to be people who make assumptions about your identity. Some of these assumptions will be positive. Others will be negative. Remember, you can't control other people. You are not responsible for managing their behavior or making excuses for their microaggressions.

As you read in Fatimah's story in the last activity, being both a racial and religious minority can cause discomfort when not acknowledged. At the same time, you may feel proud of all your identities and how they overlap. You may feel positive about being Black and Muslim, for example. Developing a healthy sense of your identities and how they intersect is essential to mental health, physical well-being, and academic success.

for you to do

Look at the illustration below. Choose two parts of your identity and, for each street, add a name that is part of your identity. For example, if you've chosen female and teen as the two parts of your identity, you'll name one street Female and one street Teen. Close to each street, list the words that you associate with that identity. For example, on the street labeled Female, you might list words like "beautiful," "nurturing," "powerful." On the street marked Teen, you might list the words "adventurous," "carefree," and "emotional."

You should now have a visual picture of two of your intersecting identities.

Were there any words that appeared on both streets? If yes, what were they?

_____

If you had to choose one identity, could you? Why or why not?

_____

_____

Share your illustration with someone you trust. Let the person know why these different parts of your identity are important. Remember your intersecting identities are what you feel and believe about yourself. It is not how others view you.

more to do

Do you think that Ayla should join the book club? Why or why not?

_____

_____

_____

What parts of Ayla's identity are being recognized? What parts are being overlooked?

_____

_____

_____

Have you ever felt that part of your identity has been marginalized (regarded as unimportant or powerless)? Explain your answer.

_____

_____

_____

Recognize that you do not have to settle for an identity as just a Black person or a girl. There are other unique parts of your identity that intersect with your race and gender.

SECTION 2

Body Image

9 my hair—my joy and my agony

Evelyn loves her hair. Her thick curls allow her a variety of styles from twists to blowouts. She religiously follows the hair-care regimen her mother has taught her. Wrapping her hair at night and sleeping on a satin pillowcase are as natural as brushing her teeth before bed. She never gives it a second thought, until her class's overnight trip to DC.

As Evelyn is unpacking her toiletries, one of her roommates comments, "You know, they have shampoo and conditioner here in the hotel room. What are you trying to do, open a salon?" Evelyn chooses to ignore the comment and continues unpacking.

Later that evening, a group of girls decides to go to a hotel pool party with a group of boys from their school. Evelyn has already been through her evening ritual and knows that getting her hair wet will ruin her hairstyle for the remainder of the trip so she chooses not to go to the party.

for you to know

How much time do you spend on your hair? It's likely that you spend more time on your hair than your White peers do. Hairstyle and care is an essential part of most Black girls' and women's routine. Some of us obsess over our hair, spend too much money getting our hair done, and have a bad day when our hair is just not right.

The history of hair in the Black community is rich and varied. For many years, straightened hair was considered more acceptable and desirable for Black women. It was desirable because it was closer to the texture of White hair, another example of how Blacks internalized White standards of beauty. Women would use hot combs and perms to achieve this look. Very kinky hair was considered "bad" hair, and straight hair was considered "good" hair. During the Black Power movement of the 1960s and '70s, natural hair in the style of an Afro was a political statement. Black hairstyles today are more a reflection of personal style and lifestyle choices. Whether you wear your hair straight, in a natural twist out, braided, in locs, or with a weave, your hairstyle is a statement about you.

Your hair is likely different from your White peers' hair. Your hair may not require washing every day. Another difference is that your hairstyle may be ruined if you get it wet. Sometimes, White peers will ask annoying questions about how you achieve certain styles. Other White peers may touch your hair because it is different. These are both microaggressions because these comments and actions show insensitivity to your reality.

Your hairstyle can influence your lifestyle choices. After spending hours getting your hair done, you may not want to swim or play a sport where you will sweat a lot and ruin your hairstyle. One choice some girls make is to wear their hair braided. Working out and sweating have less of an effect on this hairstyle.

Keep in mind that our hair is very diverse. It can range from very straight to wavy to curly to tightly coiled. Most of us have some degree of curly or coiled hair (often referred to as kinky hair).

Some Black girls experience hair dissatisfaction. When this happens, girls may spend inordinate amounts of time and money trying to get a "perfect" hairstyle. Or alternatively, they may give up and not even try to find the most appropriate and attractive hairstyle. Dissatisfaction with your hair may affect your self-esteem and body image.

for you to do

Why do you think Evelyn did not go to the pool party?

_____

_____

Think of a situation where you wanted to do something and did not because you did not want to ruin your hairstyle. Tell what happened.

_____

_____

Below are five statements about hair. Rank them from what you feel most strongly about (5) to what you feel least strongly about (1).

____ My hair is a reflection of my personal style.

____ My hair does not interfere with my daily activities.

____ I prefer my hairstyles to be low maintenance and easy to do myself.

____ I like to experiment with different hairstyles often.

____ I think wearing braids, weaves, and wigs are fun and easy ways to switch hairstyles.

Now, look at what you feel is important about maintaining a hairstyle, and what is not significant to you. This may help you decide what type of hairstyles are best suited for your lifestyle.

more to do

Have your White peers ever questioned your nightly hair routine at sleepovers or camp? Many Black girls use bonnets or headscarves to protect their hairstyles at night. Bonnets and other silk nightcaps have been around for generations, especially within the Black community. The headscarf is a rite of passage for some Black girls that starts their own hair journey. Think about your own personal hair journey. What about your hair brings you joy? Write those things on the lines in the bonnet opposite.

Choose a hairstyle that you like and that works for you. If you are involved in working out, sports, or swimming, consider a hairstyle that can withstand moisture. Consider what to say when microaggressions are made about your hair. More about microaggressions in the next activity.

10 hairstyle discrimination

Allison has been a dancer for several years. Her grandfather often jokes that she danced before she walked. She loves all dance but is most inspired by dancers of color who had broken barriers, like Alvin Ailey, Maria Tallchief, Judith Jamison, and especially Misty Copeland.

Allison cannot contain her glee when she is chosen to be Princess Florine, the same role Misty Copeland had danced numerous times. Over the next two months, Allison works harder than she has ever worked before. She becomes stronger, more poised, and more confident.

It is probably this new sense of confidence and strength that gives Allison the nerve to cut her hair. She hadn't planned on doing the big chop, but her hairdresser mentioned how much easier short hair would be to maintain. Allison thinks about how hot and sweaty she gets dancing under stage lights. She thinks about how much she hates getting perms every other month. Before she knows it, Allison is walking out of the salon with about one-inch curls framing her face.

Allison can't believe she waited so long to get this look. She even feels lighter on her feet while dancing. She loves her new hairstyle—until her dance instructor asks to speak to her after class. "What are we going to do about your hair for the performance?" Allison's happiness quickly turns to despair. She could get braids or a weave, but why are these necessary? What is wrong with her own hair?

for you to know

Black hair is beautiful, and we are seeing that celebrated now more than ever. There are countless internet tutorials and blogs dedicated to hair care and hairstyles for Black girls and women. Hair care products marketed toward Black women are on the shelves of most retail stores. But even with all this progress, you may still face microaggressions and discrimination based on your hairstyle.

Historically, some people have felt that our natural hair when it is not straightened is unclean, unkempt, and unprofessional. There have also been policies in schools, jobs, and even the US military that forbid wearing certain hairstyles like locs, twists, and braids.

Hairstyle discrimination mostly affects Black girls and women. For example, news media widely reported that Mya and Deanna Cook, twin sisters in Massachusetts, had to serve detention when school officials determined that their braids violated school policy. Another example in the news: high school cheerleader Asia Simo was kicked off the team because her hair was too thick for the "half up, half down" standard the team required for certain games.

In most states, hairstyle discrimination is legal, meaning you can be fired or required to wear your hair in a certain style. Hair discrimination mostly affects Black people, and many advocates are working on changing the laws. Even if there is not outright discrimination, many Black teens face microaggressions when they wear certain hairstyles.

As we talked about in the previous activity, Black women and girls may have a different relationship with their hair than their White peers do, so policies or microaggressions that target hair and hairstyles can feel exceptionally personal.

Microaggressions about Black hairstyles may be experienced by Black girls attending predominantly White schools. For example, if you are like Asia Simo, and you cannot wear your hair in a certain style, comments such as "Let's all wear ponytails" or "Let's all wear our hair up" are rude if your hair cannot be worn in these styles. Remember, often microaggressions are unintentional. But when comments such as these are made, they can sting.

for you to do

Regardless of how you choose to wear your hair, you may experience microaggressions or discrimination, like Allison did. Look at the comments below, and write down what you might say to each. And as always, you may decide that ignoring the comment is what is best for you.

Can I touch your hair?

Are you wearing that scarf for religion, or are you trying to be cute?

How does your hair stay that way?

Have you ever considered getting a weave?

I think you should wear your hair straight all the time.

Are dreadlocks dirty?

more to do

How do you think Allison felt when asked what should be done about her hair?

_____

_____

_____

How do you think Allison could respond to the comment made by her dance instructor?

_____

_____

_____

Tell about a situation in which you were expected to wear your hair a certain way (school, extracurricular activity, work).

_____

_____

_____

_____

You are more likely to face microaggressions about your hairstyle than outright discrimination. These are three things you can do that can help:

- Start thinking of your hair as a unique aspect of who you are and how you present yourself. Appreciate the beauty and versatility of your hair and the many hairstyle options you have.

- Respond, especially if a microaggression is made by your peers and likely to be continued if not addressed.

- Choose not to respond by recognizing but not internalizing the microaggression.

Which of these three choices do you think would work best for you? Why is this choice best for you?

_____

_____

_____

_____

_____

_____

11 what is colorism?

DeeDee is outgoing and confident, frequently surrounded by friends. She never seems fazed by the usual middle school drama. Once a classmate announced that he "would never date someone as Black as DeeDee." She quickly replied, "Don't worry, I would never date someone as ignorant as you." DeeDee is used to having to overcompensate for her skin color. And while plenty of people admire her deep tone, there is always someone who thinks her skin should be a punchline.

That's why she enjoys attending her coding class after school. Although the class is mostly White, her coding classmates never mention anything about her color. DeeDee has become friends with the only other Black girl in the class, Tasha. Tasha has also had her own negative experiences surrounding her skin tone. People often accuse her of not being Black because of her fair skin and wavy brown hair. But at coding class none of that matters, because both DeeDee and Tasha are happy there is another Black person to bond with—until one day when the girls are working on a group project to create a website.

Tasha makes an offhand comment about not using a black background because it will be hard to see the photo of DeeDee onscreen. The two White girls in the group agree and move on. But DeeDee truly feels hurt and insulted. After class, she approaches Tasha to let her know her comment felt like a rejection of her due to her skin color. What starts as a quiet conversation between friends quickly escalates. It ends with DeeDee yelling "You're nothing but a high-yella wannabe!"

for you to know

Colorism is the unfair treatment of a person based on the shade of their skin. Have you ever heard any of the following?

"She's really pretty for a dark-skinned girl."

"What are you? You're not all-the-way Black, are you?"

"Don't stay out in the sun too long. You don't want to get darker."

All these are examples of colorism. Colorism usually benefits lighter-skinned people, while disadvantaging people with darker skin. So where did these ideas about skin color come from in America? Like many hang-ups about race in this country, we have to go back to slavery to answer that question.

Enslaved women had no basic rights. Their owners would often rape them. Their children were mixed race but still slaves. Slave owners would give slaves with fairer skin "better" living and working conditions. Of course, "better" meant conditions closer to Whites. These fairer-skinned Blacks had better opportunities, nutrition, and clothing. White slave owners became more comfortable having lighter-skinned Blacks in the house. This began a long history of separating Black people according to their skin color. We are now seeing more representation from Black women of all shades, but some of the beliefs about skin color are so deep, it may take a while to dispel them.

for you to do

Both DeeDee and Tasha made negative comments about each other's skin tone. Do you think Tasha meant to hurt DeeDee? Or was this an unintentional microaggression? Write down your thoughts on DeeDee's comments about Tasha's skin tone.

_____

_____

_____

Describe an instance when you experienced colorism. If you have not experienced colorism, describe an instance when it happened to a friend or peer.

_____

_____

_____

How did it make you feel?

_____

If you or your friends have ever talked negatively about the skin color of someone else, reflect on why this is wrong.

_____

_____

_____

more to do

Loving the skin you're in and having confidence in yourself doesn't come easy. DeeDee and Tasha both had negative experiences concerning their skin color. Neither girl probably realized how sensitive the other was about this topic. That's because colorism is so deeply rooted into our culture.

Let's take a more in-depth look at the roots that cause this insecurity. The roots of the colorism tree on page 74 have been killed by words that hurt, destroy, and tear people down. Examine the words and phrases on the roots of this dead colorism tree.

Now let's create a tree with healthy roots. Use the blank spaces on the roots of the healthy tree (on page 75) to write words and phrases that focus on positive qualities individuals possess. Consider traits you love and respect in your own friends and family members. Here are some words to get you started: kindhearted, observant, giving, funny. It's up to you to plant seeds that will result in good roots and a healthy, "happy" tree.

Reflect on how your new tree is different from the old tree. How can you help plant healthy seeds with the people you meet?

_____

_____

_____

_____

_____

Although skin color may sometimes be used to describe someone, think about how negative skin-color words can hurt and humiliate. Remember to focus on peoples' positive characteristics rather than their skin color.

dealing with colorism 12

Joi is in a restaurant with her parents. A White couple sits down at the next table, and the woman compliments Joi on her looks. "You are absolutely beautiful. Your skin is flawless. You should consider modeling because dark skin is so popular right now." The man nods in agreement. Joi smiles and thanks the couple.

Her initial feeling of pride then turns to a troublesome feeling of sadness. She has conflicting thoughts. She received a compliment: that she was attractive. However, that compliment seems to assume that her beauty was just a fad or, worse, was rare because no one expected dark-skinned girls to be beautiful. While the White woman was well intentioned, her words do not make Joi feel good about her appearance. She does not enjoy the rest of her meal. She resolves to talk to her parents about this when they leave the restaurant.

for you to know

Colorism is destructive. Black girls are color shamed and face microaggressions about skin color every day. Color shaming is putting down a person of color by linking negative traits with the person's skin tone. Read the facts below. Make a mental note of any you find surprising.

- Colorism involves more than skin color. It is also prejudice based on physical traits such as hair texture, eye color, nose shape, or lip size.

- Colorism happens not only to dark-skinned people in the US but also throughout the world.

- Colorism is harmful to Blacks' mental health and contributes to feelings of low self-worth, depression, and anxiety.

- Colorism can affect Black girls' relationships with friends.

Sometimes Black girls cope with colorism in unhealthy ways. They may

- look into ways to lighten their skin;

- pay excessive attention to their personal appearance;

- always seek approval from others;

- avoid the sun to prevent their skin from darkening;

- constantly style their hair, and apply excessive makeup and other adornments, while never being satisfied with the way they look.

for you to do

Joi experienced a microaggression based on her skin color. How do you think she felt?

_____

Do you think the microaggression was intended? Why or why or not?

_____

Do you think the intention behind microaggressions matter? Why or why not?

_____

Now think about what you could say or do if you heard a similar comment. Keep in mind that responses to colorism microaggressions will take time and practice. Remember also that most microaggressions are not intentional, but they still sting. You will need to feel confident that your skin color is perfect for you. Just like with other microaggressions, you can always say nothing. After all, it is not your job to teach people how to be polite.

Joi could respond by saying "Thank you. I know many dark-skinned girls who have beautiful skin." Another response: Joi could look at her parents and remark, "Thank you. My skin color comes from my parents." What would you say, if anything?

_____

_____

Microaggressions about skin color are rude and hurtful. Practice will help you develop the skills to address them. If you do not want to respond, learn not to internalize what you hear. This means, do not let the words of others define how you see yourself. If you hear a skin-color microaggression about another person, practice speaking up. Sometimes it is easier to speak up for others than for yourself. You can also talk to your parents, another trusted adult, or a friend if you encounter a microaggression.

more to do

Think about yourself and a friend who has a different skin tone. Let's use fun and positive ways to describe your friend and you. For example, you can describe yourself as golden brown (rather than brown), or ebony (rather than dark skinned), or golden wheat (rather than light brown).

Below are some words that can be used to describe skin color to get you started. Use these words and see if you can also come up with some of your own to describe your best friend and you. Come up with two different tone descriptions for each of you.

golden brown	caramel	chocolate
ebony	copper	mahogany
espresso	chestnut	sunshine
ivory	peach	golden wheat
almond	buttermilk	amber
bronze	reddish brown	walnut brown
café-au-lait	sand colored	cocoa

My Friend	Me

Think about the words you chose. Are they fun and positive? Try thinking of different terms when referring to someone's skin color. After all, light skin, brown skin, and dark skin can get very boring, considering the hundreds of skin colors we have. If you are not already doing so, begin to think positively about your skin tone. After all, your skin is the color it is meant to be.

Maria, a Black sixteen-year-old whose parents are from the Dominican Republic, loves to go shopping with her friends. She wants to be a hairstylist or a fashion designer one day. She even has quite a few followers on her social media accounts, which feature her original fashion designs and styling choices for her hair.

Maria often posts pictures of herself alongside her friends. She has been working really hard on designing swimwear and cover-ups for their upcoming spring break. When Maria is satisfied with her beachwear designs, they are posted on social media. She is not ready for the feedback. While some of the comments are complimentary, several are not. "That cover-up isn't covering enough up." "Why do they need swimsuits? That butt is going to drag her to the bottom of the pool."

Maria knows that in the Black and the Latinx community, curves are often celebrated. How many songs has she heard talking about big butts, hips, and thighs? Clearly, the standard isn't straight and skinny. But it seems as though only a particular type of curviness is accepted—the kind of curviness that still allows for a small waist and a flat stomach. Maria is unsure how many people are blessed with this body type naturally. She certainly isn't. She looks at her wide hips and knows that her waist is not small.

for you to know

How would you describe your body? Tall, short, compact, curvy, chunky, athletic, skinny, big butt, small boobs, small waist? There are probably parts of your body that you take pride in, and some parts you don't like as much. Body image is what you see when you look in the mirror and how you feel about your body.

We have already talked about skin color and hair as part of our body image. Body type is another part of how we see ourselves. About four out of five teen girls have a concern with their body type. Comparing our bodies to others can cause dissatisfaction. The media is a significant factor in body image dissatisfaction. The majority of actresses, models, musicians, and beauty influencers are all overwhelmingly thin and White. These images convey at a subconscious level that you have to be thin to be pretty, successful, rich, or powerful.

Body shaming also contributes to body image dissatisfaction. Body shaming is when others make negative comments about someone's body. Think about these comments: "Those jeans don't look good on big girls." "Why is she going out for cheerleading?" Body shaming can lead to poor mental and physical health, such as low self-esteem, eating disorders, and avoidance of physical activity.

Not all Black girls experience body image problems. In general, Black girls are more comfortable with their bodies and do not obsess about weight as much as White girls do. Overweight Black teens are also less likely to say that they are overweight than average weight White teens. Although body image dissatisfaction may be lower for Black teens—who may be more concerned about skin color and hair—it still remains.

If you are in a predominantly White space, your body type may be different from your peers'. Black girls tend to have a heavier body weight than White girls. If you are overweight, you are more likely to be stigmatized by White than Black peers. Also, you may be considered less attractive.

Weight is not the only factor in body image dissatisfaction. The shape of your body and features such as hips and breasts, the size of your feet, or even your nose may influence how you feel about your body.

for you to do

Maria experienced body shaming on social media. These are microaggressions that we talked about in Activity 2. Have you ever been body-shamed? Tell what happened.

_____

_____

_____

How did you feel when this happened?

_____

_____

Let's think about how you could react if this type of microaggression happens again. Practicing will help you develop skills to feel more comfortable when reacting. Also, recognizing that this is a microaggression helps put it in perspective. Here are some possible responses:

- Do nothing. After all, ignorant people should be ignored.

- Comment back politely on social media that you like your body (your hair, your outfit, and so on) just the way it is.

- Block the person on your social media sites.

- Talk to a trusted friend or adult about how to respond.

Write down any other responses you can think of.

_____

_____

_____

more to do

Describe, or draw the ideal body type.

Where do you think this ideal came from: family, media, friends?

_____

How is your body type similar to others in your family?

_____

We know there are some things you can't control, such as your eyes and your height. But there are things you can control and change, like eating certain foods. Focus on what you can change in order to change your body type if this is what you want to do.

Find a recent full-body photo of yourself, or take one. Glue or tape it in the box.

Now really look at your wonderful self. Take markers, crayons, pencils, or whatever, and write down all the beautiful things you see. This is not the time to be humble. Brag about yourself and write it down! Revisit this page on those days you're not feeling so good about your body.

14 appreciating your body

Leona, a fifteen-year-old Black sophomore, is eagerly awaiting the posting of parts for the school play. This year, the spring production is a musical, where her talent would really shine. Leona feels very confident in her audition. Even people working in the auditorium had stopped to watch her on stage. Finally, the list is posted. Leona is crestfallen when she sees her name listed with the chorus. She is even more disappointed when she sees that Sarah has been cast as the female lead. Leona tries to think objectively about why Sarah would be chosen over her.

When Leona can't come up with any answers, she asks her friends what they think. Her female friends respond with the appropriate amount of shock and support, reassuring her that she is far more talented than Sarah. Her male friends, however, react entirely differently. "You just don't look the part. Sarah does," one male friend says. Another states, "You're so strong. No one would ever believe that you're a damsel in distress."

Leona looks down at her long legs, which have a lot of muscles from years of playing volleyball. She has always been praised for her tall, athletic build; it was part of the reason Leona made the varsity team freshman year. But now hearing her friends tell her that she couldn't be strong and feminine is stinging. It is the first time she begins to not appreciate her body.

for you to know

Appreciating your body means accepting your body as it is and not applying someone else's standard of what your body should look like. You will feel better about yourself, have better relationships with friends, and engage in healthier behaviors if you appreciate your body. Healthier behaviors might include more physical activity, better nutrition, and less alcohol and drug use.

Appreciating your body also means that you learn to deal with microaggressions. Microaggressions such as "You have a beautiful face," or "You need to wear makeup" can increase body image dissatisfaction and make you become less appreciative of your body. Even if you believe your whole body is beautiful, comments about your face imply that it is the only appealing part of your body. These comments could potentially change your body image satisfaction to dissatisfaction if you are not prepared for them.

Regardless of what your body looks like, it is capable of doing incredible things. Dancing, cooking, hiking, dressing up, swimming are all possible because of the body you inhabit. The purpose of your body is not to bring joy to other people, but to allow you to be purposeful and joyful. If you are not satisfied with your body, there are things you can do that may increase your appreciation. If you already feel happy with your body, use this time to reflect so you are prepared for challenges that may come in the future.

for you to do

Leona's story suggested that athletic strength was equated with a lack of femininity for Black girls, especially among males. What aspects of Leona's body were viewed negatively by her male friends?

_____

Leona's athletic build made her an excellent volleyball player. What parts of your body help you excel?

_____

Sometimes people from different racial and ethnic groups have different opinions as to what is and is not attractive. Are there aspects of your body that White peers might view more negatively than your Black peers?

_____

Check the boxes next to ways you would like to show your body love.

☐ Wear cute workout clothes.

☐ Buy an outfit you look great in.

☐ Try a new healthy recipe.

☐ Have an at-home spa day.

☐ Make up a dance to your favorite song.

☐ Exercise.

☐ Join a sports team.

☐ Say a positive affirmation while looking into the mirror.

☐ Get enough sleep.

☐ Stop talking to unkind people.

☐ _____

☐ _____

Now reflect on how you will carry out one or more of these activities. For example, if you decide you want to buy an outfit to look great in, make a plan. First, you could talk to a parent about how you can earn money to buy the outfit if you don't have the money. Two, you could identify a store to shop in. And three, you could plan a day to give yourself plenty of time to try on outfits.

I will show my body love by

_____

_____

_____

_____

_____

Make it a practice to think about ways your body serves you. Saying "thank you" to your body is one of the most important things you can do. It's not a habit that will come quickly. However, embracing your body with positive vibes will lead to more joy.

more to do

Once you start appreciating your body, you can start appreciating *all* bodies. One way to do this is to reflect on them positively. Below are images of five Black teens. Write down how you could describe them positively; for example, you could write *Person A is tall and beautiful. Person B looks like she knows how to take care of herself,* and so on.

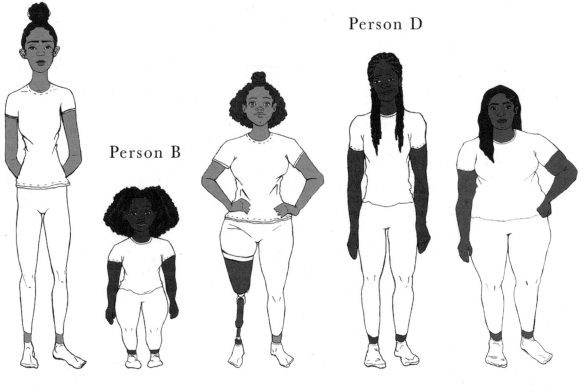

Person D

Person B

Person A   Person C   Person E

Person A _____

_____

Person B _____

_____

Person C _____

_____

Person D _____

_____

Person E_____

_____

Commit to not trying to change your body to please others unless it is also for your personal health and happiness. Commit to not judging others' bodies.

Relationships

15 who are your friends?

Ava is very excited about freshman year. For her entire life, she had gone to the school where her mother taught. Now that Ava was in high school, her parents decided she could go to the neighborhood school. She is most excited about attending school with her next-door neighbor and best friend, Sophie. Ava and Sophie have been friends since they were in preschool. They spend plenty of time at each other's homes, and now they would be classmates as well.

Sophie and Ava have the same lunch period. Sophie knows plenty of people, and their lunch table is always crowded with popular students. Ava is the only Black student in Sophie's friend group. Sophie's being White had never bothered Ava before; she thought of her as a sister. But in this environment, Ava begins to take notice of Sophie's actions and words in a new way.

One day, a boy at the lunch table makes a racial joke that Ava finds offensive. Sophie laughs along with the others. When Ava confronts Sophie about it, later, she blows Ava off, telling her that it was just a joke and that she needed to lighten up. Ava wonders if their friendship is beginning to unravel.

for you to know

Like most teens, your friends are probably very important to you. Whether you call them your friends, your BFFs, homegirls, tribe, besties, squad, crew, or posse, having relationships with like-minded people is rewarding. Everyone needs friends.

Friends support your social and emotional well-being. You share your most intimate thoughts with close friends. Friends help you develop your identity through discussions of likes and dislikes. Through sharing, you learn about yourself, gain confidence, and have greater clarity about your values and goals.

There are several types of friendships, and friends come from all walks of life:

Social media friend—Someone you have never met but share common interests and cool conversation with online.

Acquaintance—Someone you know and spend time with perhaps at school or another place, but do not spend time with outside of these places.

Family and childhood friend—Someone you've known for a long time, usually before middle school. You make these friendships through your family or your neighborhood. You have grown up and spent a lot of time together.

Good friend—Someone you communicate and hang out with frequently. You may share some personal information and talk and text on the phone.

Best friend—Someone very close who you can tell your deepest and most personal secrets to, and always count on. You trust this person and expect them to be there for you.

Two common friendship problems among teen girls are the violation of trust and unmet expectations. Have either of these happened to you? You told a friend something private, and she repeated it to others. Or you expected your friend to show up at an important event, and she didn't. In these examples, your trust was violated and expectations were not met. Knowing the type of friendships you have will help you manage expectations, and what you talk about and do together.

Black girls in predominantly White environments sometimes have challenges initiating friendships. Initiating authentic and mutually fulfilling friendships in a setting where you see yourself as different may be hard. So let's try to make sense of it all.

for you to do

You would not expect the same from a good friend as a best friend. By filling in the friendship buckets on the next page, we can see how different types of friends meet different needs.

Draw a line from each of the statements to the friendship bucket you would put it in. Some may belong in more than one bucket, but put each in the bucket you think is most appropriate.

Think about which bucket your friends are in. This will guide what you expect and how you behave with each friend.

Helping with an assignment

Talking over an argument with your parents

Choosing a formal dress for a dance

Struggling with feelings of depression

Going to a sleepover

Taking a trip together

Sharing beauty tips

Shopping together

Listening to and keeping secrets

Inviting to your party

Following on social media

Feeling like a family member

Getting nails done together

Eating lunch together at school

Visiting your home frequently

Seeing each other at basketball practice

Seeing and talking to each other often

Having lots of things in common

Being fun to be around

Sticking up for you

more to do

As with Ava and Sophie, conflict is inevitable. If a friendship is important to you, think about how to best handle a conflict. For example, Ava could have conveyed her hurt to Sophie by saying "The comment made me angry and upset," without putting Sophie down. Also think about when a relationship is worth repairing and when it is time to let it go. If a friendship is no longer mutually satisfying, it may be time to let it go.

You may have a friend you were close to but no longer share the same interests and values with. Write that person's name here.

_____

Did you change, or did your friend change? Explain.

_____

_____

_____

_____

_____

_____

16 improving your inner circle

Myra and Ella have been friends their whole lives. Their mothers are also good friends. Myra and her mother had even lived with Ella's family for a month during her parents' divorce. Even though they have very few shared interests, their friendship is a constant.

Myra is quiet. She spends most of her time tinkering in the shed behind her house, dreaming of becoming an engineer. She has a few friends, but socializing isn't that big a deal to her. Ella, on the other hand, enjoys lots of extracurricular activities. She participates in student council and drama club, and she is a cheerleader. Making friends has always come easy to her. Because she is so busy, Ella often finds herself rescheduling or canceling plans with Myra, but she assumes Myra doesn't mind. Ella knows that Myra isn't really into parties and football games.

In their sophomore year, Ella's mother is diagnosed with cancer. Ella has to significantly cut back on extracurricular activities. Her friends from cheerleading and drama club are still friendly, but she isn't invited to as many parties. Ella knows something has changed with all her friends. Well, all her friends, except Myra.

Myra still comes to the house to hang out. When chemotherapy causes Ella's mom's hair to fall out, Myra buys Ella and her mother matching headscarves. Myra and her mom even bring over chocolate chip cookie dough ice cream on Ella's birthday. Ella feels awful about the way she treated Myra earlier in the school year. She wonders why she spent so much of her time with people who were not there when she needed them.

for you to know

Now that you are a teen, you get to choose who you want to be friends with. Do you participate in an after-school activity? Are you on a dance or sports team? Friendships often start in these spaces. Friendships develop through satisfying conversations, feeling connected, and participating in activities together.

Having friends of diverse cultures, religions, racial/ethnic groups, and nationalities can enrich your experiences and bring new perspectives. Black girls at predominately White schools may struggle with making friends because their peers cannot relate to their unique experience of being a Black girl. However, some similarities and interests likely exist. Find out by starting a conversation or by attending an event together, such as going shopping or to a dance. Ask questions that convey genuine interest. For example, if you meet in a music camp, ask who her favorite musical artist is.

Think about what qualities you would like in a friend and what qualities you have that would make someone want to be friends with you. For example, if you are a good listener, show by listening attentively and asking questions.

Friends come from all walks of your life, not just school, your place of worship, or after-school and special programs. While not every acquaintance and casual friend will become a close friend, you can do some things to see if a true friendship develops. Consider participating in a Black club or organization. Think about Black dance troupes, sports teams, and social and educational programs such as Black sorority-sponsored debutante cotillions and Jack and Jill Clubs of America. Talk to your parents about this.

for you to do

How did Myra show that she was a very close friend to Ella?

_____

_____

Think about your friends. Name someone who

you trust with your innermost thoughts.

_____

offers you help before you ask.

_____

you enjoy being around.

_____

always has your back.

_____

you can disagree with and still be friends.

_____

If you named the same person for more than one of these, you have a close or even best friend. If not, don't worry. There are lots of opportunities for friendships that can eventually become close.

Having culturally diverse friends can be rewarding and educational. Identify a person who differs from you culturally who you would like to know better. What about that exchange student from Brazil who seems like a really cool person? What are some questions you might ask her? For example, you could ask her about her favorite music and foods. And what are some activities you could invite her to?

Describe the person you would like to get to know.

The person is _____

Questions I would ask are _____

_____

_____

_____

Activities I would invite her to include _____

_____

_____

_____

_____

Real friendships are mutually satisfying and bring dimensions to your life that you don't get from family. You should feel valued, liked, and respected by your friends. If you do not, consider that this is not a friend. Learning to be a good friend is essential to having good friends. Practice being a good friend every day.

more to do

To be a good friend and choose friends wisely, it is vital to identify what you value most in a friendship. While no person is perfect, there are certain things you know you want in a good friend. Let's create a recipe for friendship. Ella's recipe includes the qualities she has chosen. You may write different ingredient amounts and character traits in your friendship recipe, based on what's important to you.

Recipe For: FRIENDSHIP

Ingredients:

2 cups of compassion

1 lb of Honesty

8 tbs Respect

A dash of humor

A sprinkle of bravery

Directions:

Combine all ingredients

Stir in conversation

Let simmer over a shared interest

Enjoy!

Throughout life, you are going to try many different types of food; some you will like, some you will not. Just like the many people you will meet—some will become close friends, while others may remain acquaintances. Work to make good quality friendships. They will make your life more delicious, tasty, and fulfilling.

Recipe

For: _____

_____

Ingredients:

Directions:

_____   _____

_____   _____

_____   _____

_____   _____

_____   _____

_____   _____

17 your support squad

Janelle glances at her phone to check the time. She and her best friend, Erica, are working on posters for a community food drive. "I have to go pick up my brother and sister," Janelle explains as she gathers her things. Janelle looks around at the craft supplies strewn about and at the disappointment in Erica's face. She knows she should stay to help finish and clean up, but if she doesn't leave right away she will be late getting to her siblings' elementary school.

Janelle means to text Erica later that evening to apologize for her quick exit, but she soon forgets. She decides to take her brother and sister to the park instead of going straight home. Once she is in the house, her mom insists she practice her cello for at least an hour before dinner. After dinner, Janell has to work on her geometry homework, an assignment she thinks will take twenty minutes and ends up taking her over an hour.

It isn't until the next day, when Janelle sees Erica at school that she feels guilty for not finishing the job yesterday or reaching out the night before. Maybe if she planned her time more wisely, or was better at math or an only child, she could be a better friend.

for you to know

Is there someone you can always talk to when you feel down? Someone you seek out when you want advice on a tutor? How about someone who transports you to and from after-school programs and special events? These people all provide you with some type of social support. You could say that they are your support squad.

There is an old saying "No man is an island." This is true of women and girls too. None of us can live in a world alone. There are probably many times when you have to step up to help family and friends. You also require support from other people. You need four main types of support: academic, physical, material, and social-emotional. Teachers, tutors, librarians, and guidance counselors provide academic support. Doctors, nurses, and dentists are part of your physical support team. Providing material support means helping you with obtaining the things you need, like school lunches, clothes, and a cell phone. Most teenagers get material support from their parents, grandparents, or other family members. Last, social-emotional support comes from people who listen to your problems, show compassion and empathy, and provide advice and companionship.

Some people can provide more than one type of support. For example, a teacher might provide emotional and social support along with academic support. Your parents have probably provided all four types of support at some point.

It is important that you recognize the different people in your support squad and feel comfortable seeking the support you need. Black girls in White spaces may have difficulty identifying people they can ask for support outside of their family. They may feel that White peers or teachers cannot relate to their problems. If you feel that there is no one in your immediate surroundings, think about networks you belong to—friends of your parents, church, after-school groups, or neighbors. If you do not already have a support squad, begin working on building a strong social support system that can help you throughout life. You may be surprised at how willing people are to help. And don't be afraid to offer your support to someone in need.

for you to do

Who was Janelle providing support to?

_____

What types of support did Janelle need (academic, physical, material, social-emotional)?

_____

_____

Who could she ask for support?

_____

Think about different types of support you need. List four situations below. For example, you might need academic (help with studying for a test), physical (managing extreme menstrual pain), material (a new laptop for class), or social-emotional (dealing with online bullying). Then write the name of someone who could provide that support.

Situations Where I Need Support	Who Could Help
1.	
2.	
3.	
4.	

more to do

One way to build your support squad is to be of support to others. Support should be genuine and offered from the heart—not with conditions. Think about some things you could do to offer support to others. It could be a person or an organization. For example, you could offer to help your younger brother with a school project. You could volunteer with a local organization. Remember providing support could be a small or a large thing.

Name one person or organization that could use support from you.

_____

How could you support this person or organization?

_____

_____

_____

_____

Remember that support works both ways—even with your parents. They will likely be more willing to buy you that new cell phone if you help them with housekeeping tasks. Support should not be given grudgingly and with stipulations. Support should also be graciously accepted. Practice giving and receiving support.

18 finding emotional support

Lately, Ariana hasn't felt much like herself, but she can't quite pinpoint what the problem is. She isn't ill. Her life isn't going through any major changes. She doesn't have any conflict with her friends. But there is still something nagging at her.

At night, she sometimes can't sleep. During the day, concentration is at times difficult. Ariana has also noticed some feelings of anxiousness at the most random times, like math class and softball practice. She doesn't want to complain to her friends, because truthfully she has nothing to complain about. She knows her mother would make a huge deal out of it, and Ariana doesn't want to worry her mother. Ariana thinks about the counselor at school but quickly dismisses that idea. He primarily deals with teenage pregnancy and dropouts, not what she is experiencing. Ariana assumes her feelings will eventually go away. She doesn't want to be permanently labeled as troubled for a fleeting problem.

for you to know

Life is always going to present you with challenges. Some of these will be easy to recognize—failing a class, fighting with friends, parents' divorcing. Other challenges may not be as easy to pinpoint. It may be a feeling of uncertainty, trouble sleeping, or not being able to concentrate in school. Maybe you have completely lost interest in something you were once passionate about. You may feel sad, upset, or anxious, but not at anything in particular. The good news is that you know yourself better than anyone else, and your body will tell you when something is not quite right. Just like when you experience a fever or runny nose if your body has an infection, your body may send you signs when you are having emotional, or mental health, issues.

When you are having physical discomfort, you elicit the help of a support system— you see the school nurse, you ask your dad to pick up some medicine, you may visit a doctor, and you get extra rest and ask your friends to understand. It is important to seek support for emotional needs as well. Feelings of anxiety and sadness over a period of more than two or three weeks is a signal that you need to talk to someone about your feelings.

Blacks are less likely to seek help for mental health needs, even though many situations affect their mental health. These include racism, discrimination, and microaggressions. Black girls often get the message that they are strong and can deal with whatever is thrown at them. You may feel like you're the only person struggling with these feelings, especially if you spend most of your time in predominantly White spaces, but you are not alone. About one-third of teens report persistent feelings of sadness that interfere with usual activities over the previous year. If this is true in your case, you may need to see a therapist or counselor. Talk to your parents, a trusted adult at school, or your religious/spiritual leader about seeing someone.

for you to do

What are some of the signs that Ariana might need to talk to a therapist?

_____

_____

_____

What would you say to a friend who might be showing some of the same signs as Ariana?

_____

_____

_____

If you felt that you needed help from a therapist or counselor, identify one person you could talk to about getting this help.

_____

Practice what you would say here. For example, you could begin the conversation by saying "I have not been feeling myself for a few weeks. I am not sure what is going on but it is not getting better." If this person is not responsive, find another person to talk to.

_____

_____

_____

_____

more to do

Many resources are available to help you decide if you need professional support for mental health problems. These resources will also help you recognize if a friend needs help. One resource is the National Alliance on Mental Illness. Visit https://www.nami .org/Your-Journey/Teens-Young-Adults to see what they offer for teens. Reflect on ways you can use the information on this site.

_____

_____

_____

_____

_____

_____

_____

SECTION 4

Institutions

19 my family is different

Tabithah is excited about the upcoming weekend. She and other members of her dance team are planning on spending Saturday night at Avery's house after their competition. She hasn't asked her parents yet, but she is sure it will be fine. The girls have known each other for years, and her parents have met Avery's parents several times.

Tabithah forgets to mention it to her parents until Friday evening when she is packing her bag for her dancing competition. She is shocked when her mother says she isn't allowed to go.

"But why not?" Tabithah practically begs her mother.

"Avery's parents are just a little too relaxed for me," her mother says. "I don't feel comfortable letting you spend the night."

It is true that Avery has way different rules at her house than Tabithah does. Avery is allowed to drink as long as she is at home with parental supervision. She and her brothers are also allowed to have guests spend the night, and everyone just camps out in the den. But Tabithah has no interest in drinking or in hooking up with anyone. To Tabithah, it seems like Avery's parents trust her, but her own parents are determined to treat her like a young child forever.

for you to know

Do your parents need to know where you are every minute of the day and night? And though you love your little sister, why does she have to hang out with you? After all, she is four years younger. To make matters worse, your grandmother just moved into your room, so you now have to share a room with your sister.

Sound familiar? Black families have these and similar dynamics more so than White families. Every family is unique, but Black families have some common features and dynamics. Do any of these resonate with you?

- Your parents monitor your activities and have more rules than your White peers' parents.

- Your family is multigenerational. Your grandparents, aunts, uncles, and even great-grandparents may live in the same house as you.

- Your parents expect you to look after your younger sibling. After all, your older cousin looked out for you.

- You call someone aunt or uncle, although they are not biologically related or related by marriage.

- Your mom is the head of your house. Over 50 percent of Black children are raised in mother-headed households. Although you may not live with your father, he connects with you by phone, visits regularly, and takes you out.

- Your parents expect you to attend church or another worship service at least once a week, sometimes more frequently.

If one or more of these scenarios fit your family, your family is typical for a Black family. The families of your White peers may differ. They may be monitored less, have fewer rules, and make more independent choices. Also, their household is more likely to have two parents or stepparents.

There is no right or wrong family. Each family has a culture that dictates behaviors and norms. Black parents know that sometimes you are in spaces that are not welcoming. They know the challenges awaiting you in society. They know that if you get in trouble the consequences will be worse for you than for your White peers. They want to help you thrive in a system stacked against you.

for you to do

Do you think Tabithah's parents are being too strict? Why might they be hesitant to allow her to sleep over?

_____

_____

_____

Why do you think Black parents tend to have more rules than White parents?

_____

_____

_____

Black families tend to have a broad view of the family. The family includes not only immediate family but also people such as play cousins, Mom's best friend, and church members. List some of the people who feel like family to you whether or not they are biologically related or related by marriage.

Name of family member	How is this person related to you?
Sonya Brown	My mother's best friend
Theresa Williams	Grandmother

This exercise allows you to think about some of the people you consider family. These are the people you talk to and hang out with, who help you with money and other things you need, care for you, and love you.

more to do

Sometimes parents' rules seem arbitrary. But if you dig a bit deeper, you'll find that they are rooted in a desire to help you thrive. Look at the people you just listed, and choose an older family member to interview, preferably a grandmother, grandfather, or someone at least one generation older than your parents. Here are some questions you could ask. You can also come up with your own questions. Before beginning the interview, be sure to ask this person if it is okay to record them.

Do you think it is easier being a parent now or when you were raising your kids? Why?

What values did you try to instill in your children?

What rule did your kids hate the most?

How did you discipline your children?

What were your most significant concerns for your children when they were outside your home?

Listen to the interview. The comments will help you understand your parents. Think about how the answers impacted them and, in turn, you. On the next page, create something that represents your family's beliefs about parenting and family. The space is blank so your creation can be as unique as your family. You can write a poem or song, draw a picture, make a collage, or embellish some photographs. Just try to capture whatever was most significant in your interview.

Your parents learned their values from their parents and other family members. Remember, your parents have to deal with not only caring for you but also keeping you safe in ways that White parents do not usually worry about. This is not fair, but it is a reality for Black people in this country.

Use this space to create the results of your interview.

communicating with parents about being black 20

Sasha just turned fifteen and a half, which means that she and her twin brother, Stephen, can get their learners' permits. Their dad takes them to the DMV, and both emerge with smiles, gripping their new IDs in their hands. "I guess I don't need to ask if you passed," Dad says jokingly.

Sasha and Stephen have both been to driver's education and are anxious to get on the road so they can start clocking their hours behind the wheel. Their dad gives them lots of opportunities to practice driving. And although the twins weren't usually competitive, it drives Sasha crazy that Stephen is a better driver than she is. Her brother teases her every time she gets behind the wheel.

One day it is Sasha's turn to practice the drive to school. On the way, she is pulled over by a cop. Her father had forgotten to put on the new registration sticker. Sasha immediately becomes nervous and is visibly shaking. Luckily, her dad is in the passenger seat and handles the talking. The officer is friendly enough, and Sasha is let go without even a warning. But she can't get herself together afterward. She asks Stephen to drive the rest of the way to school.

Once they are at school, Sasha can't stop thinking about the morning drive to school. Even her friend Emily notices that she was distracted in class. "What's wrong?" Emily asks. Sasha doesn't know what to say. She doubts that Emily would understand her anxiety attack caused by being pulled over. No, this is definitely a problem that will have to be addressed with family and family only.

for you to know

Did you know that most Black teens encounter at least one act of discrimination every month? Others experience numerous microaggressions weekly. This means you spend a lot of time and energy thinking about and processing how to respond to racially charged incidents, even if they are not actually racially charged as was the case with Sasha. This time could be used to do more constructive things.

Your White peers and their parents do not have to think about racial microaggressions and discrimination. Black parents worry about their children being locked up in jail, injured, and worse. They worry about everyday slights and discrimination their children face. To counter this, many Black parents "racially socialize" their children. This means they talk to their child about what it means to be Black in this country. Here are some of the messages Black parents give their children. Have you heard any of these?

- Be sure to be really polite if you are stopped by a police officer. Keep your hands where the officer can see them.

- Stay away from specific neighborhoods.

- Know that because you are Black you will not always be treated fairly.

- You need to be twice as good to get half as much.

- You must always act in a certain way even if your White peers do not; for example, no loud talking, use of curse words, or running.

Your parents socialize you to prepare you for racism and discrimination. They may also socialize you to be proud of your Black heritage by exposing you to positive Black influences. Many White parents of Black children also socialize their children about being Black. However, if they do not because they have not had the personal experiences of a Black person, ask them to connect you with a trusted Black adult (for example, a family or neighborhood friend) who can share personal experiences. It is essential to be aware of all facets of being Black in America.

for you to do

Why do you think Sasha was reluctant to speak to her White friend about being pulled over?

_____

_____

_____

Have you or someone close to you encountered a situation like Sasha where you felt afraid of the police or another authority figure? Write down what happened.

_____

_____

_____

_____

How did you feel afterward?

_____

_____

_____

_____

Every interaction may not be a point of conflict; however, microaggressions also impact your well-being. Have your parents discussed with you how to handle microaggressions from an authority figure (for example, a store clerk watching you closer than your White peers)? If so, what did they tell you? If not, write down all the questions you'd like to ask them.

_____

_____

_____

_____

_____

_____

_____

more to do

It is essential to be able to communicate your feelings to your parents or another trusted adult. By letting them know what is happening, they can help the situation by calming you, speaking to someone about it, or encouraging you on what to say. If your gut tells you something is not right about any situation you are in, you should talk to your parents or another trusted adult.

The racialized situations you find yourself in can be infuriating, frustrating, and sometimes scary. It can also be uncomfortable to discuss these situations. You may feel like you are reliving the situation each time you talk about it.

The flowchart below can help guide your conversation with an adult. Use it as a tool to help you feel more in control when these types of situations occur. Think about Sasha's experience and how she might use this chart; then you can work through your own if a situation comes up. Discuss with your parents.

Remember, your parents and extended family are your biggest allies. They have likely experienced similar situations. Talk to them about how they handled these situations. Tell them what happened as soon as you can after it occurred so that you will not forget the details. Sometimes people who say hurtful things do not intend for their words to be harmful. Other times, people are intentionally racist and discriminatory. Your family can help you decide which is which, and whether and how to respond.

Am I physically safe?

No

Get to safety.

Call for help

- Develop a quick way to text a trusted adult.
- Discuss the situation once you feel safe.

Walk/drive away

- Keep going until you are at a safe distance.

Bring attention to yourself

- Look for possible allies.
- Explain your situation.
- Stay with them until you are safe.

Yes

Take deep breaths.

Am I emotionally able to handle this?

Yes

Articulate your concern.

Is the person receptive?

Yes   **No**

STOP

Make a record of what happened.

No

Walk away.

Say: I would like to handle this with my parent/coach present.

Seek advice from a trusted adult.

whose history? not seeing yourself in school lessons 21

Olivia enjoys history. She especially likes finding out about contributions Blacks have made throughout history. She is looking forward to the discussion of Blacks during her Advanced Placement history class. To her dismay, only a few minutes are spent discussing the transatlantic slave trade. This discussion focuses on the selling and buying of Africans by Europeans.

Olivia is aware of how enslaved Africans were treated. She is also mindful of how many of them made contributions to this country even while enslaved. Her teacher makes no mention of these contributions. When the teacher covers the period of the civil rights movement, there is only a brief discussion that mostly focuses on Dr. Martin Luther King.

Olivia has all sorts of feelings. She likes her teacher and enjoys participating in class discussions. However, she feels cheated by the limited focus on Blacks. She thinks she has missed out on an essential part of her history.

for you to know

Throughout the history of the United States, there have been significant contributions from people of color, women, LGBTQ+, and people with disabilities. However, many schools spend most of their allotted time teaching and discussing contributions of White men. Ignoring or downplaying the role that Blacks and other diverse people have is a microaggression. There are several reasons why you may not learn a diverse perspective of United States history.

1. Lack of resources. Educational materials do not include adequate information on the history of all people in the United States.

2. Lack of knowledge. Teachers may not know much about Black history.

3. Lack of time. Teachers must prioritize what needs to be taught. A state test may include questions about Benjamin Franklin instead of Benjamin Banneker.

4. Discomfort. Teachers may be uncomfortable teaching topics about race.

Regardless of the reasons, it can be challenging to sit in a classroom without seeing yourself represented in the curriculum. Students who see themselves represented in the curriculum are more engaged, connect to the material better, and achieve better results. If your school does not provide instruction that represents you, you are still able to learn about your history and culture.

Often schools and teachers that teach Black history do so within the context of enslavement and civil rights. The history of Black people in this country is not limited to fighting for freedom or civil rights. In school, White students get to see themselves as authors, inventors, doctors, artists, engineers, and statesmen. Black students don't see themselves reflected in all these areas.

After you take the following quiz, go back and highlight the names of people you learned about *in school*.

for you to do

The purpose of this quiz is to demonstrate contributions Blacks have made. Match each of these Black heroes to their accomplishment. (See answers at the end of this activity.)

Matthew Henson _____

1. Hand carved a clock believed to be the first built in the US and designed the layout for Washington DC streets

Madam C. J. Walker _____

2. One of only two American women to win the Nobel Prize in Literature

Ida B. Wells _____

3. Part of the first team to travel to the North Pole

Charles Drew _____

4. First self-made female millionaire in the US

Benjamin Banneker _____

5. Developed large-scale blood banks used in World War II

Katherine Johnson _____

6. First woman to run for the Democratic Party's presidential nomination

Shirley Chisholm _____

7. First American woman to win three gold medals in the 1960 Olympics

Wilma Rudolph _____

8. First female National Security advisor

Condoleezza Rice _____

9. Journalist who toured Europe to teach about violence in America (mostly lynching)

Toni Morrison _____

10. Mathematician whose calculations helped put the first Americans in space

more to do

There are ways that you can incorporate your history and culture into your school day. Look at the activities below, and circle at least one that you may be able to accomplish.

When given a choice for a book report or history project, intentionally choose a Black female author or subject to study.

With your teacher's or school counselor's permission, audit a class on Black history given by a university or online.

Discuss with a trusted faculty member starting a Black student association as an extracurricular activity.

During class discussions, ask teachers directly how Blacks (or women) contributed to this topic.

Answers to Quiz

Matthew Henson, 3; Madame C. J. Walker, 4; Ida B. Wells, 9; Charles Drew, 5; Benjamin Banneker, 1; Katherine Johnson, 10; Shirley Chisholm, 6; Wilma Rudolph, 7; Condoleezza Rice, 8; Toni Morrison, 2.

representing yourself 22

Janelle is passionate about being a journalist. She spends her summers attending writing camps. During the school year, Janelle is a producer on her school's weekly podcast, which focuses on current events. She is excited about this Wednesday's meeting because she emailed Mr. Townsend, the faculty advisor, a great story idea. Janelle wants to cover the climate change rally scheduled for the weekend. She wants to interview some activists as well as listen to the speeches. To produce a balanced show, Janelle also wants to speak with protesters.

On Wednesday, Janelle is shocked when Mr. Townsend passes out everyone's assignments. The climate change rally has been given to David. Janelle is assigned the opening of the Jackie Robinson baseball field at the local park. The local NAACP has been working on renaming the field, which had previously been named after a Confederate general. While Janelle does not like the assignment, she does not know how to tell Mr. Townsend.

for you to know

We have already discussed how a lack of representation can affect you at school. Another common challenge occurs when a Black student is expected to represent the entire Black race; for example, when you are asked what Black people think about a particular topic. It also occurs when others expect your interest and activities to be primarily Black focused to the exclusion of other interests. It can be frustrating to have to explain Blackness to people, especially adults. It adds a layer of stress that White students don't experience. It robs you of your individuality.

During your teens, you are figuring out who you are as an individual. By now, your tastes in music, movies, and food are uniquely yours and probably differ from your parents' tastes. In addition to your personal tastes and preferences, your moral alignment and ethical boundaries are being defined. This is a time to explore your feelings about political and global issues. It is not a coincidence that so many social movements started with adolescents. You may experience stress, anger, or sadness when teachers and others do not recognize your unique interests and experiences, and assume you are like all others in your racial group.

for you to do

Janelle's teacher expects her to write about the experiences of Black people simply because she is Black. While the teacher's intentions may be good, situations like the one above can place unnecessary stress on students.

Are there things your classmates or even teachers consider Black things? Make a list of them here.

_____

_____

_____

_____

Can you think about a time when you were in a situation like Janelle's? Write about it here.

_____

_____

_____

_____

How did you feel when this happened?

_____

_____

Janelle's situation is another example of a microaggression. You always have the option of addressing microaggressions head on, if you feel safe and comfortable doing so.

Here are some openers you can use the next time you find yourself in one of these situations. Fair warning: it takes practice to put these sayings into your own voice.

- Is there a particular reason you're asking me that question?

- I am not an expert on…

- I can only speak for myself, and I believe…

- In my experience,…

- My personal interests are…

Reread Janelle's story. Think about what she might say to Mr. Townsend. Write down the possible responses on these lines.

_____

_____

_____

_____

_____

more to do

A coat of arms serves two purposes. First, it shows the world your unique interests, talents, and cultures. Are you interested in gardening? Astronomy? Black history? Math? Fashion design? Poetry? Think about what excites you and what you could do all day.

A coat of arms is also a shield—a shield that can be used to protect you when needed.

Design your own coat of arms. You can draw it on a blank piece of paper or use this outline.

Refer to your coat of arms often as a reminder of your unique interests and talents. Try to stay true to what you love to do and are good at.

media stereotypes 23

Kayla is a typical fourteen-year-old eighth grader. Most weekends, she spends time with her friends, listening to music, going to the movies, or just hanging out at someone's house watching TV. Recently Kayla and her friends started watching a reality show called *A Date by Prom.* It is kind of like *The Bachelor,* except it takes place in a high school.

"I think he should choose Brianna," says Kayla's friend Bailey. "She's an athlete, and he's an athlete, so they have a lot in common."

"No way. He should choose Emma," someone else chimes in. "She does all that volunteer work."

Kayla and her friends begin to debate over which girl would be best for the handsome quarterback to date. Everyone has a different opinion. He should date the cheerleader...no, the student council president...or maybe the foreign exchange student.

"Well, I bet we can all agree that there's no way he's going to pick Imani."

All of Kayla's friends nod in agreement.

"Absolutely not."

"Remember the time she yelled at Emma for borrowing her brush."

"And in the pool party episode, she just sat on the side talking about how much she hated swimming."

Kayla feels a bit uncomfortable. She agrees that Imani seems like an awful person. However, as the only Black there, Kayla almost feels like she is betraying Imani by not speaking up for her. On the other hand, maybe there is another cause for her discomfort, but she cannot pinpoint what.

for you to know

We interact with the media every day on our phones, TVs, and computers. Mass media is designed to communicate with a large group of people. Today, people use social media, TV, and even billboards to spread specific messages. But art, books, movies, and music are also forms of media.

The images of Black women in the media began long before the internet or even TV. Images of the Mammy have been in books in the United States since slavery. Mammy was a large woman with a jolly smile and a head scarf, usually red. An enslaved African woman named Sara Baartman was put on display in Europe so white Europeans could stare at her large buttocks, similar to how we might look at animals in a zoo. These stereotypes were developed by the White media, which has profited from presenting Black women in a certain way.

Today, some Black girls and women use these stereotypes too. We want you to become familiar with the stereotypes most frequently used to describe Black girls and women. We also want you to reflect on how the media may impact the way you see and present yourself. Think of a rapper who dresses very sexily and continually talks about her body. She might be using these stereotypes to sell more records and get exposure.

There are four common stereotypes used to describe Black women in the media: angry Black woman, sassy sidekick, caretaker, and exotic beauty. They show that black women exist mainly to please others. Stereotypes put humans into one single box. They do not allow people to show their many different selves.

Take, as an example, the angry Black woman stereotype. All of us get angry, but the stereotype of the angry Black woman takes away all the other emotions you are entitled to express. Have you ever remained quiet, to avoid being a stereotype? This activity will help you embrace your authentic self and all the characteristics you possess—thereby challenging stereotypes.

for you to do

Read about each of these stereotypes on the left of the page. On the right, give examples of when you have seen these stereotypes. Remember to think about movies, TV shows, music, and advertisements.

Stereotype	Example
Angry Black woman: Black women are loud, quick-tempered, and challenging to get along with. They are always ready to get into a fight, orally or physically.	
Sassy sidekick: Black women exist to give helpful advice and friendship to the main character. They never have their own experiences or story line.	
Caretaker: Usually older Black women, caretakers are typically maids or nurses whose world is centered on caring for a White person.	
Exotic beauty: While there is nothing wrong with being seen as beautiful, the exotic beauty stereotype suggests that Black women have nothing else to offer. This stereotype usually focuses on the differences between Black bodies and bodies of other races. The beauty of all Black bodies is not appreciated.	

more to do

Being able to put a name on a stereotype helps us recognize it for what it is. It reduces our negative feelings about ourselves when we hear it. Have you heard of other stereotypes used to describe Black girls or women? If so, what are they?

_____

_____

Have you ever remained quiet to avoid being a stereotype? Maybe you swallowed your anger so nobody would call you an angry Black girl. Perhaps you wore certain clothes to prevent anyone from commenting on your body. How does it make you feel? Look at the example, and draw your own picture in the box on the next page.

You can defy stereotypes by defining and presenting yourself based on *your* characteristics. Name four characteristics that define you. These may be based on your personality (for example, outgoing, shy, optimistic). They may also be based on your interests and talents (for example, plays the piano, good at soccer, likes to draw).

1. _____

2. _____

3. _____

4. _____

5. _____

Ask someone you trust to give you four characteristics that define how they see you. Compare their list to yours, using a Venn diagram.

How I see myself

How we both see me

How my friend sees me

Think about other actions you can take to present more of yourself to the world (for example, I can join the debate club; I can participate in more art shows at school).

Write down your ideas here:

_____

_____

_____

_____

_____

_____

_____

24 shielding yourself from stereotypes

Zoey is a fifteen-year-old biracial high school freshman. Inspired by Sophia Coppola, Kathryn Bigelow, and Ava DuVernay, she dreams of being a filmmaker one day. Zoey and her friends love going to the movies and go a few times a month. They watch everything from horror to romantic comedy. Sometimes they even go to the local independent film house and watch foreign films or old classics. After watching, she and her friends usually discuss and critique the movie over burgers and fries.

One Friday morning, Zoey's best friend, Natalie, meets her at her locker and asks, "What time should we all meet tonight?" Zoey isn't surprised that her friends want to see *Emancipation on Hold,* the new Johanna Williams movie. It looks amazing, and she wants to see if herself. The movie stars some of her favorite actors. And it is so infrequent that there are movies made by female directors, much less a Black female director, Zoey considers it her duty to support the film. She just doesn't want to see the movie with her friends.

Zoey always feels uncomfortable watching movies about slavery around her White friends. In most of the movies they see, Blacks are the sidekicks, if in the movie at all. It seems as though the only time Blacks are featured on the screen, it is depicting their pain and suffering. Zoey doesn't want her friends to discuss slavery over burgers and fries. She doesn't want to get overly emotional in the theater. And even worse, she doesn't want to see her friends have no emotional reaction to the suffering of people who look like her.

Zoey cannot share all these thoughts with Natalie. Instead, she says, "How about seven?"

for you to know

In the previous activity, you read about four stereotypes commonly applied to Black girls and women. There are a few reasons why seeing or hearing these stereotypes might make you uncomfortable:

- You may feel pressure to live up to one of these stereotypes. This may make you feel like you are performing for others.

- You may suppress your own feelings and emotions to avoid being seen as one of these stereotypes.

- You may worry about what your friends think about you when one of these stereotypical images is presented.

All these responses are natural. However, feelings of discomfort can negatively impact your mood, your relationships, and eventually your mental health. That is why it is so important to know how to deal with these media images when you encounter them. It is impossible to avoid movies, music, and TV. It is also not practical to avoid media while you are with your friends. Going to the movies, listening to music, and discussing TV is part of any teen's social life. However, you do not have to be uncomfortable. This activity will help you recognize and deal with stereotypes.

for you to do

The first step to defying stereotypes is to identify their impact on you. Take a few moments to really think about what you are watching and listening. Think about how you feel after listening to certain songs or watching certain shows that portray Black girls and women negatively.

List three specific examples of media that make you uncomfortable.

    1. _____

    2. _____

    3. _____

List three specific examples of media that make you feel better afterward.

    1. _____

    2. _____

    3. _____

What would happen if you were to stop watching or listening to the media that make you uncomfortable? Circle all that apply.

I would be left out of conversations with my friends.

I would not be able to watch TV with my family.

I would fall behind in a class.

I would have more time for schoolwork.

Nothing would happen to me at all.

I would be a happier person.

Reflect on what you circled. Perhaps if you stopped watching or listening to the media it would not be as bad as you thought.

Are there any media outlets that support your authentic self? Maybe it's the world of crafters on social media or home bakers on the Food Network. List them here.

_____

_____

_____

Write down what you are looking for in the media content you consume, then tell how you can search for it. For example, are you looking to gain information about a particular topic? Are you looking for entertainment? Are you interested in listening to a certain artist?

_____

_____

_____

more to do

The chart that follows shows how a person might react to negative media images of Black women and girls. Circle a stereotype you are familiar with. Next, circle how the image makes you feel, and then what actions you would take.

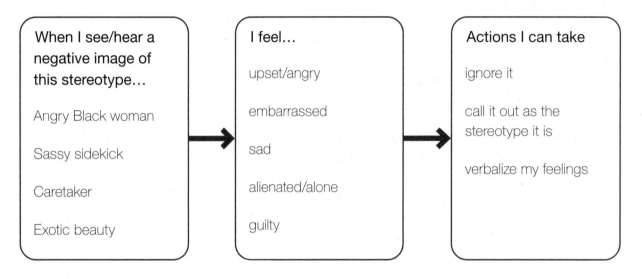

When I see/hear a negative image of this stereotype…	I feel…	Actions I can take
Angry Black woman	upset/angry	ignore it
Sassy sidekick	embarrassed	call it out as the stereotype it is
Caretaker	sad	verbalize my feelings
Exotic beauty	alienated/alone	
	guilty	

Identify one person you feel comfortable talking to about this. Share this chart with them. If it is someone who lives in your household, develop a list of healthy media habits with them. If you feel comfortable enough with your friends to speak up and you think they would be willing to listen, talk to them about how you feel when you hear negative stereotypes. For a movie with a negative portrayal of a Black woman, here is how you might start the conversation: "Seeing [name of Black woman] depicted as angry and aggressive makes me uncomfortable because most Black women I know don't act that way."

How would saying something like this make you feel?

_____

_____

Juliana knows she needs to get to math class. But instead of rushing to class, she is staring at her phone with disbelief. A classmate has sent her a link to a video from a party she was at over the weekend. She had gone with her best friend, Ruth, who was the star of this video. They told each other everything...well apparently not everything. Ruth hadn't mentioned sneaking away to an empty room with Scott, or anything else on this video.

Juliana spends the day wondering how she will comfort her friend about the unflattering video circling around on social media. But on their walk home, Juliana realizes she was worried for nothing.

"I can't study with you Wednesday," Ruth begins. "I made plans." She continues, "It's only been a few days since I posted the video from the party, and I already have plans for the next two weeks. Now everyone knows that I'm not just some science geek."

"You posted the video!" Juliana is practically screaming. "You are *not* that girl in the video. People are going to be disappointed when they find out you really are just some science geek." Ruth shrugs as she walks away. "It's the internet. I can be whatever I want."

for you to know

If you are like most teens, you use social media daily. Here are just some of the things teens say about social media.

- It gives me a platform to express my opinions.

- It allows me to interact with people from all over the world.

- It pressures me into posting a certain type of lifestyle.

- It keeps me connected to my friends and support system.

- It is a way for other teens to bully me.

- It can keep me informed, but it is also full of drama.

As you can see, there are both positive and negative things about using social media. Social media is a tool; use it when it is helpful for you. Think of this: If you wanted to hang a picture on the wall, a hammer and nail would be the perfect tools to use. But if you were trying to slice a cake, not so much. Thinking about social media through this lens might help you maintain a balance.

There are lots of negative consequences for teens who are constantly on social media. Oversharing, sleep deprivation, and FOMO are all consequences of being overly dependent on social media. As a Black girl, you are more likely to see content about race and racism. This content can be a useful tool, helping to educate you and motivate you for action. Or the constant messaging about racism might make you feel stressed, fatigued, or even depressed (the equivalent of slicing a cake with a hammer).

No one would ever expect you to stop using social media altogether. You should, however, use it in a way that adds value to your daily life. These four tips can help you maintain a healthy relationship with social media and a balanced life.

- Limit the amount of time you spend on social media; aim for less than three hours a day.

- Carefully consider what you're posting and who you are responding to. Challenge yourself to live in the positive zones of the internet.

- Talk to other people about your social media usage. Ask if your online persona is an accurate representation of who you are in person. If it is not, ask yourself how it differs. And how is this persona benefiting you?

- Think before you post. If it's personal, think twice.

for you to do

Juliana's friend Ruth posted a video. What might be some consequences of her post? (Remember, consequences can be positive or negative.)

_____

_____

_____

What types of things do you post on social media?

_____

_____

_____

Reflect on how you use social media, using the four tips above. Is your use of social media consistent with these tips? If not, is there something you might change?

_____

_____

_____

more to do

There are many positive ways to use social media. For each of these purposes, write down what platform you would use and who the post is intended for. For example, if you were demonstrating a new cheerleading routine, you could post it on YouTube. The post would be intended for other teens interested in cheerleading.

Purpose	Platform (TikTok, Instagram, YouTube, etc.)	Audience (friends, followers, influencers)
Organizing a party at your house		
Selling a product/craft		
Advocating for social change		
Sharing fashion/makeup/other advice		
Demonstrating a skill you have mastered		
Developing a challenge to uplift other Black girls		

Now review this chart. Choose one thing you would like to develop further. Focus your social media usage for two weeks building on that idea. Remember, social media is a good tool when it is used for the right task. And just like any other tool, it can be damaging when not used appropriately.

26 posting and following with good intentions

Gigi considers herself an activist. She goes to rallies, she boycotts offensive brands, and she educates her friends on how to be more socially conscious. Unsurprisingly, Gigi uses social media to show support for the many different causes she supports: #ABLM #animalshavesouls, #feminism, #internationalcitizen, #equalityforeverybody. She has built up quite a following that includes a few celebrities. One evening, Gigi is going through her feed and sees this message:

I am shocked that you would post this piece of racist propaganda. Clearly, I misread your message this entire time.

There are a dozen more replies on this thread, most expressing how much they disagree with the article. A couple of messages are far more personal and derogatory.

Gigi realizes that this response was to an article link she had posted. The headline read "The Real Reason Black Lives Matter." Gigi had only skimmed the first few lines before posting, so she decides to go back and read the article in its entirety. The article is full of sarcasm and spite toward Blacks. Her stomach begins to sink. Each hateful remark feels like a personal insult to her Blackness.

for you to know

Using social media in a responsible manner means not only being aware of the content you produce, but of who you choose to repost and follow. When you show support for something, it is a reflection of you.

Therefore, when you post, do so with good intentions. Like Gigi, you may be eager to post something related to Black justice. You may simply want to let your friends and family know what you are up to. Or you may want to share a new dance routine you just learned. Whatever you post, be mindful that others will see, and perhaps judge, you based on your post.

Make sure that whatever you post reflects who you are, your beliefs, and your attitudes. Before you post, also think about the following: *Does my post offend anyone? Am I sharing too much personal information? Is the content irrelevant or of little interest to others? Am I posting to boast about myself?* If the answer to any of these is yes, consider not posting.

When you post something you regret, you can wait it out and avoid responding to comments. You can also reflect on the post and whether you need to apologize. If you offend someone, you can apologize for them being offended, even if you believe your opinion is valid.

Just as what you post affects how others see you, who you follow affects how you feel and see yourself. Do you follow friends and peers? Family and relatives? Celebrities? Influencers? Have you ever been active following others on social media and found yourself feeling bad about yourself at the end of the day? Perhaps you checked out your friends' posts, and then you began to obsess about what you could post that would make you look good. Perhaps you are following a celebrity who is beautiful and has a perfect life (at least as seen on social media). You are reminded of your imperfect life. When you read about the positive experiences of others, it is natural to compare your experiences, even without knowing the full details of theirs or how much is true. Whomever you follow, consider how you feel after visiting their site. If you feel positive and uplifted, continue to follow. However, if you feel unattractive, anxious, or helpless, do not follow.

If you are in a predominately White space, following White friends and peers may be valuable in keeping you connected and abreast of what is going on. However, if you are constantly comparing your appearance and your life to theirs, the differences might lead to negative thoughts about yourself. Follow anyone who uplifts you, particularly those whose posts display understanding of your life experiences as a Black person.

for you to do

What do you most often post about on social media?

_____

_____

_____

Write about a time you regretted a post.

_____

_____

_____

_____

Reflect on how you could have better handled it.

_____

_____

_____

_____

more to do

Let's take a look at three people or brands you follow on social media. Write the person/brand in the top row of this chart. Then put an X in the space that corresponds to the reason or reasons you follow this person/brand. For example, if you follow your aunt, you would put the X next to personal connection. If this aunt were also famous, you might put another X next to celebrities.

Reasons	Person/Brand 1	Person/Brand 2	Person/Brand 3
Content or information			
Aesthetics			
Number of followers			
Personal connection			
Celebrities			

Look at the reasons you choose to follow people/brands. Are they aligned with your personal beliefs and goals? If you are using social media to build your brand, the number of followers becomes very important. For staying connected with family and friends, a personal connection might be your priority. Write down three goals for using social media.

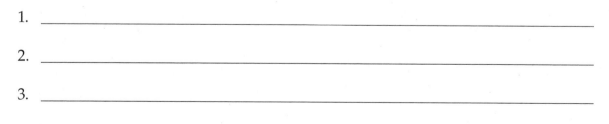

1. _____

2. _____

3. _____

conclusion: be who you are

Dear Brilliant Black Girl,

We see you, thriving in a space not necessarily built for your success. We hope that by using the strategies in this workbook you feel armed with the knowledge to tackle microaggressions, discrimination, and other challenges. You have so much beauty and strength inside you, and you are never alone on this journey. Consider this workbook the beginning, and go out into this world empowered to make your mark on the world.

Remember the three goals we had at the beginning of this journey.

You are seen.

You are knowledgeable.

You are empowered.

And one more:

You are loved.

Love,

Dr. Faye, Angela, and Ivy

acknowledgments

We owe a debt of gratitude to Austin Miles, who created most of the images for this workbook. The images you created brought our ideas to light and strengthened our engagement with Black girls. The love and support of the Belgrave and King families and the Walker, Patton, and Ka-Re families encouraged us while we worked on this project. We are grateful to Asani Ka-Re (daughter of Angela Patton), who taught us much as she continues to navigate White spaces. Our editor at New Harbinger, Jennye Garibaldi, sold us on the need for this book and supported its development every step of the process. Thank you, Jennye. We also appreciate Karen Schader, a very experienced copy editor, who provided constructive feedback and thorough editing of our work.

Faye Z. Belgrave, PhD, is professor of psychology and founding director of the Center for Cultural Experiences in Prevention at Virginia Commonwealth University. The Center has implemented several interventions targeted at reducing problem behaviors and strengthening healthy behaviors among African American girls and young adults. Belgrave is the first author of cultural curriculums for African American girls (Sisters of Nia) and boys (Brothers of Ujima). Sisters of Nia helps girls ages eleven to fourteen embrace their culture and develop fulfilling relationships, while learning skills to navigate risky situations. It has been favorably reviewed in several peer-reviewed journals, and is one of a few cultural curriculums specifically targeting African American girls. Belgrave has published extensively on topics related to African American psychology.

Ivy Belgrave has been an educator for more than two decades. She has taught in the United States and abroad. Currently she lives in the Cayman Islands. Outside of the classroom, Belgrave has worked with girls focusing on racial identity and social and emotional development. Belgrave cofounded and led CREATE (Culturally Responsive Education and Advocacy Together for Equity) for teachers at a previous school, and has trained teachers on the tools of cultural proficiency. Belgrave is a member of the Society of Children's Books Writers and Illustrators.

Angela Patton is CEO of Girls For A Change (GFAC). She was recognized in Richmond, VA's *Style Weekly* in 2015 as a Top "40 under 40," and listed in a national coalition of girl-serving groups that identified GFAC as one of five programs to note. In 2016, President Obama recognized Patton as a White House Champion of Change for after-school programming for marginalized girls of color. In 2018, GFAC was recognized as Nonprofit Partner of the Year, and in 2019, the *Richmond Times-Dispatch* nominated Patton for Person of the Year. Patton was appointed to the Virginia STEM Commission, and selected to participate in the Omega Women Residency Leadership program for women leading nonprofits for women and girls. Patton is available for speaking engagements, trainings, panels, and consulting services on Black girls and other girls of color.

Foreword writer **Lauren Christine Mims, PhD**, is assistant professor of educational psychology at Ball State University. Mims' work focuses on promoting the well-being and development of Black students. Mims was appointed assistant director of the White House Initiative on Educational Excellence for African Americans by President Barack H. Obama.

More ⏱ Instant Help Books for Teens

An Imprint of New Harbinger Publications

THE SELF-LOVE REVOLUTION

Radical Body Positivity
for Girls of Color

978-1684034116 / US $16.95

YOUR LIFE, YOUR WAY

Acceptance and Commitment Therapy
Skills to Help Teens Manage Emotions
and Build Resilience

978-1684034659 / US $17.95

**REAL TALK ABOUT SEX
AND CONSENT**

What Every Teen Needs to Know

978-1684034499 / US $17.95

**THE ANXIETY WORKBOOK
FOR TEENS,
SECOND EDITION**

Activities to Help You Deal
with Anxiety and Worry

978-1684038633 / US $17.95

THE RESILIENT TEEN

10 Key Skills to Bounce Back from
Setbacks and Turn Stress into Success

978-1684035786 / US $17.95

**THE TEEN GIRL'S
SURVIVAL GUIDE**

Ten Tips for Making Friends,
Avoiding Drama, and Coping
with Social Stress

978-1626253063 / US $17.95

�',️ new**harbinger**publications

1-800-748-6273 / newharbinger.com

(VISA, MC, AMEX / prices subject to change without notice)
Follow Us 🔲 🇫 🐦 ▶️ 📌 in

Don't miss out on new books in the subjects that interest you.
Sign up for our Book Alerts at **newharbinger.com/bookalerts** 🖱️